TONY BUZAN

Tony Buzan is the originator of Mind Maps™, the President of The Brain Foundation, Founder of The Brain Trust and the Use Your Head Clubs, and the creator of the concept of Mental Literacy.

Born in London in 1942, Tony Buzan graduated from the University of British Columbia in 1964, achieving double Honours in Psychology, English, Mathematics and the General Sciences. In 1966 he worked for the *Daily Telegraph* in Fleet Street and edited the *International Journal of MENSA* (the high IQ Society).

As one of the world's leading authors, he has published 20 books (19 on the brain, creativity and learning and one volume of poetry), His books (which include: *Use Your Memory, Make the Most of Your Mind, Speed Reading, Buzan's Book of Genius and Mental World Records* and *Get Ahead*) have now been published in 50 countries and translated into 20 languages. *Use Your Head*, his classic BBC Book, has surpassed worldwide sales of a million.

Tony Buzan has become an international media star featuring in, presenting and co-producing many satellite broadcasts, television, video and radio progammes, both national and international, including the record-breaking *Use Your Head* series (BBC TV), the *Open Mind* series (ITV), *The Enchanted Loom* (a one-hour feature documentary on the brain), and numerous talk shows. His two latest videos are *MindPower*, distributed by BBC Video, which teaches the concepts of Mind Mapping for business use, and which won a top award at the 1991 IVCA Festival, and *If at First . . .*, a new way of looking at how to transform failure into success.

He is advisor to government departments and multinational organisations (including BP, Barclays International, Digital Equipment Corporation, Electronic Data Systems, Hewlett-Packard, and IBM), and is a regular lecturer to leading international businesses, universities and schools. Among members of the Young Presidents' Organisation he has become affectionately known as 'Mr Brain'. He is Founder of the Memoriad, the World Memory Championships, and co-Founder of the Mind Sports Olympiad, the 'Mental Olympic Games'. Much of his work is devoted to helping those with learning disabilities. He is also the holder of the world's highest 'creativity IQ'.

Tony Buzan is an advisor to international Olympic coaches and athletes and to the British Olympic Rowing Squad as well as the British Olympic Chess Squads. He is an elected member of the International Council of Psychologists and a Fellow of the Institute of Training and Development. He is a Member of the Institute of Directors, a Freeman of the City of London, and is also a Patron of the Young Entrepreneurs' Societies of both Cambridge and Bristol Universities. Adding to his list of honours, including the YPO Leadership Award, was his recent recognition by EDS with the Eagle Catcher Award — given to those who attempt the impossible and achieve it!

ALSO BY TONY BUZAN

Books

Use Your Memory
The Mind Map Book: Radiant Thinking
Speed (and Range) Reading
Master Your Memory
Memory Visions (workbook for *Master Your Memory*)
The Brain User's Guide
Make the Most of Your Mind
Harnessing the ParaBrain
   (Business version of *Make the Most of Your Mind*)
Spore One (poetry – limited edition)

Videotapes

Use Your Head
The Enchanted Loom
Buzan Business Training
Family Genius Training
Mind Power
If at First . . .

Audiotapes

Learning and Memory
The Intelligence Revolution
Make the Most of Your Mind
Supercreativity and Mind Mapping
Buzan on the Brain
Buzan on Memory
Buzan on Reading
Buzan on Radiant Thinking & Creativity
Buzan on Success
Buzan on Body and Mind

Other Works

The Universal Personal Organiser
'Body and Soul' (Master Mind Map poster)
The Mind Map Kit
Master Your Memory Matrix (SEM^3) 0–10,000
The Brain Club Manifesto
The Brain Club Magazine

see *Appendix* for more information, including how to order these items

use your HEAD

TONY BUZAN

BBC BOOKS

DEDICATED TO YOU

**and to my beloved Mum and Dad,
Jean and Gordon Buzan**

External Editor-in-chief: Vanda North

With thanks to all those whose effort and
co-operation enabled me to write this book:

Zita Albes; Jennie Allen; Astrid Andersen;
Jeannie Beattie; Nick Beytes; Mark Brown; Joy Buttery;
my brother, Barry Buzan; Bernard Chibnall;
Carol Coaker; Steve and Fanny Colling; Charlotte Crace:
Susan Crockford; Tricia Date; Janet Dominey;
Charles Elton; Lorraine Gill; Bill Harris;
Brian Helweg-Larsen; Thomas Jarlov; Trish Lillis;
Hermione Lovell; Annette McGee; Joe McMahon;
Vanda North; Khalid Ranjah; Pep Reiff; Auriol Roberts:
Ian Rosenbloom; Caitrina Ni Shuilleabhain;
Robert Millard Smith; Sarah Spalding:
Chris and Pat Stevens; Jan Streit; Christoper Tatham;
Lee Taylor; Nancy Thomas; Sue Vaudin; Jim Ward;
Bill Watts; Gillian Watts; Phyllida Wilson.

© Tony Buzan 1974, 1982, 1989, 1995

First published 1974
Revised and extended edition published 1982,
reprinted 1983 (twice), 1984, 1985 (twice), 1986, 1987 (twice)
Hardback edition first published 1984
Revised edition published 1989
Reprinted 1989
Reprinted 1990, 1991 (twice), 1992
Reprinted 1993
Reprinted 1994
This revised edition published 1995
Reprinted 1995, 1996

Published by BBC Books an imprint of
BBC Worldwide Publishing
BBC Worldwide Ltd., Woodlands,
80 Wood Lane, London W12 0TT

Set in Univers 9/11 by Phoenix Photosetting
Printed and bound in Great Britain by
Redwood Books, Trowbridge

ISBN 0 563 37103 X (paperback)

Contents

Our 21st Birthday

This special 21st birthday edition of *Use Your Head* marks the 21st anniversary of spring 1974, when *Use Your Head* was published, the *Use Your Head* ten-part television series was first aired, and the basic concepts of *Mind Maps* were first formally introduced to the world. To mark the occasion, the biggest celebration ever held for a book – the Carnival of the Mind, a 21st 'coming out' birthday party – is being held at the Royal Albert Hall in London on 21 April 1995.

The *Use Your Head* saga started in 1973, when BBC executives and the author met to plan a book and television programme series that would offer the first Operations Manual for the brain. Both were such an immediate success that the television series was repeated regularly for ten years, and the book became a worldwide best seller, launching Tony Buzan on a major new career and a non-stop schedule of global travel.

By the end of the 1970s, the first success stories were being reported, especially the amazing, inspirational story of Edward Hughes (see page 11). In the early 1980s the first of an on-going series of super lectures to large bodies of students were being given. Among the most notable of these was the 'Soweto 2000' event in Johannesburg, South Africa, when 2000 teenagers from the township of Soweto attended, voluntarily, a three-day *Use Your Head* spectacular. By the end of the 1980s, *Use Your Memory* had expanded the concept introduced in Chapter 5 of *Use Your Head* into an entire dictionary of memory techniques – and the annual sales of *Use Your Head* continued to rise, approaching the magical one million mark.

In the early 1990s the *Mind Map Book: Radiant Thinking*, son of *Use Your Head*, was published, and the Brain Trust, the charity based on the principles outlined in *Use Your Head*, was formed. It took as one of its major initiatives the formation of public Use Your Head clubs for anyone with a brain who wanted to learn how to use it and already numbers thousands of members.

Introduction

Hamlet: *What is man,*
If his chief good and market of his time
Be but to sleep and feed? a beast, no more.
Sure, he that made us with such large discourse,
Looking before and after, gave us not
That capability and god-like reason
To fust in us unused.

HAMLET: Prince of Denmark
Act IV, Scene IV   A plain in Denmark

Use Your Head is written to help you do just that. By the time you have finished the book you should understand much more about how your brain works and how to use it to the best advantage, be able to read faster and more efficiently, to Mind Map more effectively, to solve problems more readily and to increase the power of your memory.

This introductory section gives general guide lines about the book's contents, and the way in which these contents are best approached.

THE CHAPTERS

Each chapter deals with a different aspect of your brain's functioning. First the book outlines the most up-to-date information about the brain and then applies this information to the way in which your vision can be best used.

The fifth chapter explains how you can improve memory both during and after learning. In addition a special system is introduced for the perfect memorisation of listed items.

The middle chapters explore your mind's internal 'maps'. This information about how you think is applied to the way in which you can use language, words, imagery and Mind Maps for recording, organising, remembering, creative thinking and problem solving.

The ninth chapter deals with the new Mind Map Organic Study Technique which will enable you to study any subject ranging from English to Higher Mathematics, Philosophy to Languages.

The final chapter summarises the gigantic leaps made in the last fifteen years, gives a new perspective on the ageing brain and leads you into new directions for the future.

In the colour section you will find Mind Maps which you are advised to look at before and after reading each relevant chapter — they serve as a preview/review summary.

In certain of the chapters, important key concepts are printed in bold type to enable your easy reference in previewing and reviewing.

YOUR EFFORT

It is essential that you practise if you wish to be able to use effectively the methods and information outlined. At various stages in the book are exercises and suggestions for further activity. In addition you should work out your own practice and study schedule, keeping to it as firmly as possible.

PERSONAL NOTES

At the end of each chapter and at the end of the book you will find pages for 'Personal notes and applications'. These are for any jottings you might wish to make during reading and can also be used when you discover further information and applications after you have 'finished' the book.

BIBLIOGRAPHY

On page 151 you will find a special list of books. These are not just books of academic reference, but include books which will help you develop your general knowledge as well as giving you more specialised information concerning some of the areas covered in *Use Your Head*.

YOU AND YOURSELF

Use Your Head is designed to help you to expand as an individual, so that through an increasing awareness of yourself you will be able to develop your own ways of thinking.

Each person using information from this book starts with different levels of learning ability, and will progress at the pace best suited to him. It is important therefore to measure improvement in relation primarily to yourself.

Although much of the information has been presented in connection with reading, formal noting and studying, the complete application is much wider. When you have finished and reviewed the book, browse through it again to see in which other areas of your life the information can be helpfully applied.

1 A Use Your Head tale: an impossible dream – the Edward Hughes story

THE BEGINNING

After *Use Your Head* was first published in 1974, a 'fairly average student, middle of the form, not doing particularly well in any subject' took, in 1982, at the age of 15, his 'O' level examinations.

His results, as expected, and as they had always been, were C's and B's. He was disappointed with the results because he had set his heart on going to Cambridge University and realised that if he carried on academically the way he was, then he didn't stand a chance.

The student's name was Edward Hughes.

A little while later Edward's father, George, introduced him to *Use Your Head*, and armed with new information about himself, and about how to Mind Map, learn and study, Edward went back to school revitalised and motivated. He announced that he was going for A's in all his subjects, and that he definitely wanted to be put forward for Cambridge.

The reaction of his teachers was understandably bemused and varied. 'You can't be serious: come on, you've got no chance – your academic results have never been anywhere *near* the standard which Cambridge requires,' said one.

'Don't be daft! You could possibly get a B, but you'll probably get a C,' said the second. When Edward said he wished to take not only the standard exam, but also to write the Scholarship paper, the master said flatly, 'No, it's a waste of the school's money and your time entering for that exam. We don't think you'll pass, for the exams are very, *very* difficult – we don't even get many passes from our best candidates.' After Edward persisted, the school was willing to put him forward, but he had to pay his own £20 entrance fee in order not to 'waste the school's money'.

The third teacher said that he had been teaching the same subject for the last twelve years, that he was the expert in the area, and that he knew what he was talking about when he said that Hughes would only get a B or a C. The teacher named 'another chap' who was a much better student than Edward, and said that Edward would never be as good as the other. As Edward said at the time, 'I disagreed with his reading of the situation!'

The fourth teacher chuckled, said he obviously admired Edward's ambition, said that Edward's dream was possible but unlikely, said that even if he worked hard he'd only get a B, but wished him luck and said that he always liked someone who showed a bit of in-itiative.

'I WILL GET AN A'

To each of the teachers, and to anyone who questioned his goals, Edward's final response was always simply: 'I will get an A.'

The school initially did not want to put Edward's name forward for Cambridge, but after a while agreed to do so, letting the colleges at Cambridge know that they didn't really think that this particular student was likely to get the place for which he applied.

The next and immediate stage was the college interviews. At these, the Cambridge dons informed Edward of the school's opinion of him, agreed with the school that his probability of success was very low, admired his initiative, told him that he'd need at least two B's and an A, but more probably two A's and a B, or three A's, and wished him luck.

Still undaunted, Edward pursued a plan of *Use Your Head* and physical training. In his own words: 'I was getting nearer the exams. I summarised my last two years of school notes neatly into Mind Maps. I then coloured them, highlighted them, and produced giant Master Mind Maps for each of the courses, and in some instances for each major section of each course. In this way I could see where and how the more detailed elements fitted together, and in addition get a good overview, thus enabling me to be able to "just flick through" giant sections of the course with completely accurate recall.

'I kept reviewing these Mind Maps once a week, and as it got nearer to the exams, even more regularly. I practised my Recall Mind Maps, not looking at my books or other notes, simply drawing from my memory what knowledge and understanding of the subjects I had, and then comparing these Mind Maps with my Master Mind Maps, checking the differences.

'I also made sure that I had read all the main key books, and then sorted these down to a few, read them in depth, and Mind Mapped them so that my understanding and memory were maximised. In addition I studied good essay form and style, and used my own Mind Maps as a basis for practising essay and examination writing.

'I accompanied this by getting fitter, by running two to three miles, two to three times per week, getting lots of fresh air, doing lots of press-ups and sit-ups, and working out in a gym. I became better physically, which I found helped my concentration enormously. As they say, healthy body, healthy mind; healthy mind, healthy body. I felt better about myself and I felt better about my work.'

THE EXAMINATIONS – THE RESULTS

Eventually Edward sat four examinations: Geography, the Geography Scholarship paper, Business Studies and Mediaeval History.
His results were as follows:

Subject	Mark	Rank
Geography	A	Top student
Geography Scholarship	Distinction	Top student
Mediaeval History	A	Top student
Business Studies	A and 2 Distinctions	Top student ever

Within a day of the publication of the results, Edward's first-choice college at Cambridge had confirmed his place, and accepted his request for a 'year off' to see a bit of the world before he started his University career. During his year's 'sabbatical' he worked in Singapore, as a cowboy in Australia and also had a holiday in Fiji and Hawaii. He then flew across to California where he worked in embryo transfer units and on cattle ranges. He worked his way across America on farms, and then returned to England.

Before going to Cambridge, Edward decided that, in addition to academic success throughout his time at University, he would set himself the goals of creating a new student society, playing lots of sports for the college, making many new friends, and basically having 'a tremendous time!'

AT CAMBRIDGE

In sports he was immediately successful, playing in the college soccer, tennis and squash teams. And in the area of student societies he might even be termed an over-achiever. For in addition to founding the Young Entrepreneurs Society, the largest of its kind in Europe, he was asked to preside over the Very Nice Society, a charitable society of 3,600 members, which grew to 4,500 under his presidency – the largest society in the history of the University. In view of his work for these two societies, the other society presidents asked Edward to form and preside over a society for presidents. This he did and became the President of the Presidents Club!

Academically he first studied the habits of the 'average student' and reported: 'They spent about 12–13 hours reading for each essay, linearly noting all the information they could, reading all possible books, after which they'd spend 3–4 hours writing the essay itself (some students would actually rewrite their essays, occasionally spending an entire week on one essay).'

In view of his experience with the 'O' level preparation and examinations, Edward decided to allocate himself 2–3 hours a day, 5 days a week, to study. 'During those three hours I went to a key lecture, summarising all the relevant information in Mind Map form. I set myself the goal that as soon as any essays were set, I'd go away and do a Mind Map on what I knew about the subject or what I thought was relevant. And then leave it for a couple of days, think about it, turn it over in my mind, and then speed and range read the relevant books, Mind Mapping the relevant information from them. I'd then take a break or do some exercise, and then come back and do a Mind Map on the essay itself. Having completed my essay plan, I'd take another break, and then sit down and complete the essay *always* within 45 minutes. With this technique I regularly achieved high marks.'

Before the final Cambridge examinations, Edward worked to a schedule virtually identical to that with which he prepared his 'A' levels, and took six final examinations.

The results?

THE RESULTS

In the first, he was given a pass, normally considered fair but here excellent because 50% of those taking the examination failed it, and no firsts were given; in the second, third and fourth, three 2.1's; and in the final exams two first classes – not only first classes, but *Star Firsts*, the highest marks in the University for that subject.

Immediately after graduation, Edward was offered employment as a Strategic Thinker for a multi-national entrepreneurial company, a job described by the University as 'one of the best ever' for a Cambridge undergraduate. As Edward summarised: 'Cambridge was fantastic. I was fortunate enough to get a lot out of it – a lot of friends, a lot of experience, a lot of physical activity, a lot of enthusiasm for and success in academia, and three years of absolutely great enjoyment. The major difference between myself and the others was simply that I knew how to think – how to use my head. I was a C and B student before I knew how to "get an A". I did it. Anyone can.'

(Reader: do *you* have a Use Your Head tale? If you do, please send it to Tony Buzan c/o address on page 149.)

2 Your mind is better than you think

MAN'S UNDERSTANDING OF HIS OWN MIND

Since I wrote the introductory chapter on the brain for the first edition of *Use Your Head* in 1974, research in that area has been exploding with new and exciting discoveries. Rather than stating, as I did then, that 'only in the last 150 years' has the bulk of progress been made in this area, I can now state that only in the last *fifteen* years has the bulk of our knowledge been accumulated. This seems extraordinarily late when you consider that life appeared on earth 3,500,000 years ago. Bear in mind, however, that mankind has only known the *location* of its brain for the last 500 years. In some ways this is not surprising. Consider for a moment that you have no idea where your brain is to be found, and a friend asks: 'Where is the centre of your feelings, emotions, thoughts, memories, drives and desires located?'. You, like most others (including Aristotle!) might quite rationally decide that your brain was located in the heart and stomach area, because that is where you experience the direct physical manifestation of mental activity most regularly and dramatically.

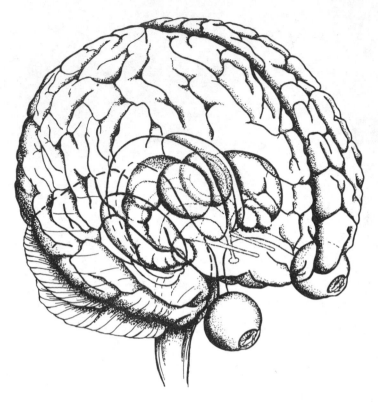

Fig 1 The brain
Source: SCIENTIFIC AMERICAN (see page 150 for details)

If, even now, as we pursue with computers and electron microscopes what must be the most elusive quarry mankind has ever chased, we must still admit that the sum total of the knowledge we have acquired today is probably less than 1% of what there is to know. Just when tests seem to prove that the mind works in a given way, along comes another test which shows another picture, or along comes another human being with a brain who manages to make us need to rework the whole frame.

What we are gathering from our efforts at the moment is a knowledge that the brain is infinitely more subtle than we had previously thought, and that everyone who has what is ironically called a 'normal' brain has a much larger ability and potential than was previously believed.

A few examples will help to make this clear.

Most of the more scientific disciplines, despite their apparent differences of direction, are all being drawn into a whirlpool, the centre of which is the brain. Chemists are now involved with the intricate chemical structures that exist and interact inside our heads; biologists are uncovering the brain's biological functions; physicists are finding parallels with their investigations into the farthest reaches of space; psychologists are trying to pin the mind down and are finding the experience frustratingly like trying to place a finger on a little globule of mercury; and mathematicians who have constructed models for complex computers and even for the Universe itself, still can't come up with a formula for the operations that go on regularly inside each of our heads every day of our lives.

MORE THAN ONE BRAIN

What we *have* discovered during the last fifteen years is that you have two upper brains rather than one, and that they operate in different degrees in the different mental areas; that the potential patterns your brain can make is even greater than was thought at the end of the 1960s, and that your brain requires very different kinds of food if it is to survive, *see fig 2* (overleaf).

In Californian laboratories in the late 1960s and early 1970s, research was begun which was to change the history of our appreciation of the human brain, and which was eventually to win Roger Sperry of the California Institute of Technology a Nobel Prize and Robert Ornstein worldwide fame for his work on brain waves and specialisation of function, carried on through the 1980s by Professor Eran Zaidel and others.

In summary, what Sperry and Ornstein discovered was that the two sides of your brain, or your two cortices, which are linked by a fantastically complex network of nerve fibres called the Corpus Callosum, deal dominantly with different types of mental activity.

In most people the left cortex deals with logic, words, lists, number, linearity, and analysis etc, the so-called 'academic' activities. While the left cortex is engaged in these activities, the right cortex is more in the 'alpha wave' or resting state, ready to assist. The right cortex deals with rhythm, imagination, colour, day-dreaming, spatial awareness, Gestalt (whole picture) and dimension.

Subsequent researches showed that when people were encouraged to develop a mental area they had previously considered weak, this development, rather than detracting from other areas, seemed to produce a synergetic effect in which all areas of mental performance improved.

Professor Zaidel continued Sperry's work at the University of California with some startling results. He discovered that each hemis-

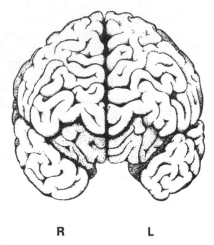

R	L
rhythm	words
spatial awareness	logic
Gestalt (whole picture)	numbers
imagination	sequence
day-dreaming	linearity
colour	analysis
dimension	lists

Fig 2 Front view of the two sides of the cortex (looking at you) and their dominant processes
Source: L. GILL

phere contains many more of the 'other side's' abilities than had been previously thought, and that each hemisphere also is capable of a much wider and much more subtle range of mental activities.

At first glance history seemed to deny this finding however, for most of the 'Great Brains' appeared very lopsided in mental terms: Einstein and other great scientists seemed to be predominantly 'left-cortex' dominant, while Picasso, Cézanne and other great artists and musicians appeared to be 'right-cortex' dominant.

A more thorough investigation unearthed some fascinating truths: Einstein failed French at school and numbered among his activities violin playing, art, sailing, and imagination games!

To his imagination games Einstein gave credit for many of his more significant scientific insights. While daydreaming on a hill one summer day, he imagined riding sunbeams to the far extremities of the Universe, and upon finding himself returned, 'illogically', to the surface of the sun, he realised that the Universe must indeed be curved, and that his previous 'logical' training was incomplete. The numbers, equations and words he wrapped around this new image gave us the Theory of Relativity – a left *and* right cortex synthesis.

Similarly the great artists turned out to be 'whole-brained'. Rather than note books filled with stories of drunken parties, and paint slapped haphazardly to produce masterpieces, entries similar to the following were found:

'Up at 6 am. Spent seventeenth day on painting number six of the latest series. Mixed four parts orange with two parts yellow to produce a colour combination which I placed in upper left-hand corner of canvas, to act in visual opposition to spiral structures in lower right-hand corner, producing desired balance in eye of perceiver.' – Telling examples of just how much left-cortex activity goes into what we normally consider right-cortex pursuits.

In addition to the researches of Sperry and Ornstein, the experimental evidence of increased overall performance, and the confirming historical fact that many 'Great Brains' were indeed using both ranges of their capacity, one man in the last thousand years stands out as a supreme example of what a human being can do if both cortical sides of the brain are developed simultaneously: Leonardo da Vinci. In his time he was arguably the most accomplished man in *each* of the following disciplines: art, sculpture, physiology, general science, architecture, mechanics, anatomy, physics, invention, meteorology, geology, engineering and aviation. He could also play, compose and sing spontaneous ballads when thrown any stringed instrument in the courts of Europe. Rather than separating these different areas of his latent ability, he *combined* them. Leonardo's scientific note books are filled with 3-dimensional drawings and images; and equally as interesting, the final plans for his great painting masterpieces often look like architectural plans: straight lines, angles, curves and numbers incorporating mathematics, logic and precise measurements.

It seems, then, that when we describe ourselves as talented in certain areas and not talented in others, what we are *really* describing is those areas of our potential that we have successfully developed, and those areas of our potential that still lie dormant, which in reality could, with the right nurturing, flourish.

The right and left cortex findings give added support to the work you will be doing on memory systems, on note taking and communication, and on advanced Mind Mapping, for in each of these areas it is essential to use *both* sides of your upper brain.

INTERCONNECTIONS OF THE BRAIN'S 'LITTLE GREY CELLS'

Dr David Samuels of the Weizmann Institute estimated that underlying the brain's basic range of activities, between 100,000 and 1,000,000 different chemical reactions take place every minute!

In your brain there are a minimum of 1,000,000,000,000 individual neurons or nerve cells. This figure becomes even more astounding when it is realised that each of your neurons can interact with from 1 to 100,000 other neurons in many ways. At the time I was writing the first edition of *Use Your Head* in 1974, it had been recently estimated that the number of permutations might be as many as 1 followed by 800 noughts. To realise just how enormous this number is, compare it with a mathematical fact about the Universe: one of the smallest items in the Universe is the atom (*see fig 6, page 24*). The biggest thing we know is the Universe itself (*see fig 5, page 23*). The number of atoms in the known Universe is predictably enormous: 10 with 100 noughts after it. The number of possible thought-maps in *one* brain makes even this number seem tiny. *See figs 3 and 4 (opposite).*

Shortly after the first edition of *Use Your Head* was published, Dr Pyotr Anokhin of Moscow University, who had spent the last few years of his life studying the information processing capabilities of the brain, stated that the number one followed by 800 noughts was a gross under-estimation. The new number he had calculated was conservative due to the relative clumsiness of our current measuring instruments in comparison to the incredible delicacy of the brain. The number was not one, followed by 800 noughts. The pattern-making capability of the brain, or 'degrees of freedom' throughout the brain is

'so great that writing it would take a line of figures, in normal manuscript characters, more than 10.5 million kilometres in length! With such a number of possibilities, the brain is a keyboard on which hundreds of millions of different melodies – acts of behaviour or intelligence – can be played. No man yet exists or has existed who has even approached using his full brain. We accept no limitations on the power of the brain – it is limitless.'

Use Your Head is written to help you play your virtually infinite mental keyboard.

Other examples of the mind's abilities abound – examples of extraordinary memory feats, feats of super-strength, and unusual control of body functions defying the 'laws of science', are becoming more widespread. They are now fortunately more documented, generally recognised and usefully applied.

```
10,000,000,000,000,000,000,000,000,000,000,000,000,
000,000,000,000,000,000,000,000,000,000,000,000,000
000,000,000,000,000,000,000
```

Fig 3 The number of atoms (one of the smallest particles we know of) in the known Universe (the largest thing we know of). *See text on facing page.*

```
10,000,000,000,000,000,000,000,000,000,000,000,000,
000,000,000,000,000,000,000,000,000,000,000,000,000,
000,000,000,000,000,000,000,000,000,000,000,000,000,
000,000,000,000,000,000,000,000,000,000,000,000,000,
000,000,000,000,000,000,000,000,000,000,000,000,000,
000,000,000,000,000,000,000,000,000,000,000,000,000,
000,000,000,000,000,000,000,000,000,000,000,000,000,
000,000,000,000,000,000,000,000,000,000,000,000,000,
000,000,000,000,000,000,000,000,000,000,000,000,000,
000,000,000,000,000,000,000,000,000,000,000,000,000,
000,000,000,000,000,000,000,000,000,000,000,000,000,
000,000,000,000,000,000,000,000,000,000,000,000,000,
000,000,000,000,000,000,000,000,000,000,000,000,000,
000,000,000,000,000,000,000,000,000,000,000,000,000,
000,000,000,000,000,000,000,000,000,000,000,000,000,
000,000,000,000,000,000,000,000,000,000,000,000,000,
000,000,000,000,000,000,000,000,000,000,000,000,000,
000,000,000,000,000,000,000,000,000,000,000,000,000,
000,000,000,000,000,000,000,000,000,000,000,000,000,
000,000
```

Fig 4 In the late 1960s it was calculated that the number of different patterns the 1,000,000,000,000 individual nerve cells of the brain could make was 1 followed by 800 noughts. Recent estimates have shown that even this number is too small! *See text on facing page.*

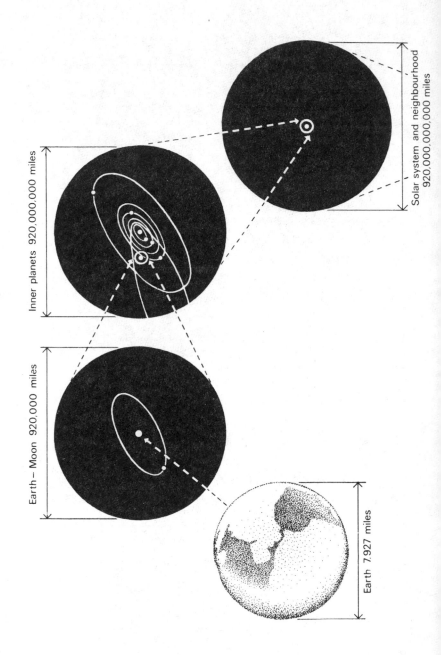

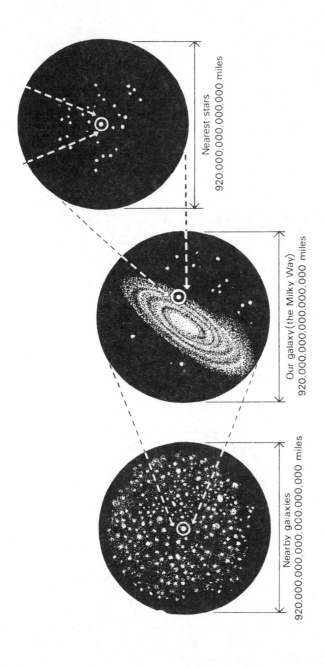

Fig 5 The enormous size of the known Universe. Each successive black sphere is a thousand million times (1,000,000,000) as big as the one before it. *See text on page 20.*

Nearest stars
920,000,000,000,000 miles

Our galaxy (the Milky Way)
920,000,000,000,000,000,000 miles

Nearby galaxies
920,000,000,000,000,000,000,000,000,000 miles

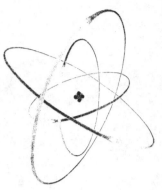

Fig 6 The atom – one of the tiniest entities known. In the tip of a person's finger there are many billions of atoms, and in the entire Universe a number equal to 10 with 100 noughts after it.
For the relationship between these facts and the brain's interconnecting networks, see figs 3 and 4 (page 21) and text on page 20.

MODELS OF PERCEPTION: EYE – BRAIN – CAMERA

First let us consider the eye/brain/mind system: as recently as the 1950s the camera provided the model for our perception and mental imaging: the lens of the camera corresponded to the lens of the eye, and the photographic plate to the brain itself. *See fig 7 (opposite).* This conception was held for some time but was very inadequate. You can confirm this inadequacy by doing the following exercises: in the way that one normally does when day-dreaming, close your eyes and imagine your favourite object. Having clearly registered the image on your inner eye, perform the following activities.

Rotate it in front of you

Look at it from the top

Look at it from underneath

Change its colour at least three times

Move it away as if it were seen from a long distance

Bring it close again

Make it gigantic

Make it tiny

Totally change the shape of it

Make it disappear

Bring it back

These feats can be performed by you without much difficulty; the apparatus and machinery of a camera could not even begin to perform them.

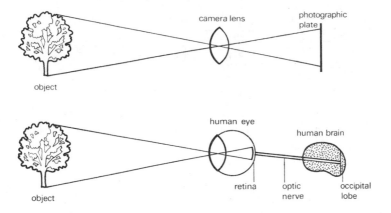

Fig 7 Contrary to earlier thought the brain operates in a much more complex manner than the camera. *See text on page 24.*

THE HOLOGRAM AS A MODEL FOR THE BRAIN

Recent developments in more refined technology have fortunately given us a much better analogy: the hologram.

In this technique, an especially concentrated light or laser beam is split into two. One half of the ray is directed to the plate, while the other half is bounced off the image and then directed back to the other half of the ray. The special holographic plate records the millions of fragments into which the rays shatter when they collide. When this plate is held up in front of the laser beams directed at special angles towards it, the original image is recreated. Amazingly, it is not recreated as a flat picture on the plate, but is perfectly duplicated as a three-dimensional ghost object that hangs in space. If the object is looked at from above, below or the side, it is seen in exactly the same way as the original object would be seen.

Even more amazingly, if the original holographic plate is rotated through 90 degrees, as many as 90 images can be recorded on the same plate with no interference.

And to add still further to the extraordinary nature of this new development, if the plate is taken and smashed to smithereens with a hammer, each particle of the shattered plate will, when it is placed in front of the specially directed lasers, still produce the complete three-dimensional ghost.

The holograph thus becomes a far more reasonable model than the camera for the way in which your brain works, and begins to give us some idea of just how complex an organ it is that we carry about with us.

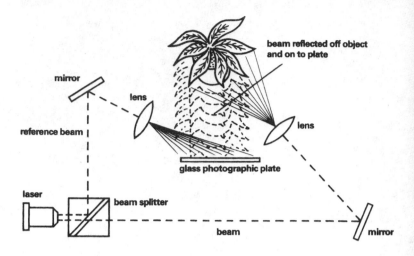

Fig 8 The holograph – a more appropriate model for your multi-faceted brain.

But even this extremely refined piece of technology falls far short of the unique capabilities of the brain. The holograph certainly approximates more closely the three-dimensional nature of our imaginations, but its storage capacity is puny compared to the millions of images that our brains can randomly call up at an instant's notice. The holograph is also static. It cannot perform any of the directional exercises of the kind described on page 24 which the brain finds so easy and yet which must involve the most unimaginably intricate machinery. And even if the holograph were able to accomplish all this, it would not be able to do what our minds can: to see its own self, with eyes closed, performing the operations!

IQ AND YOUR NATURAL BRILLIANCE

They say that IQ tests measure our 'absolute intelligence' so therefore *they* must be right. Apart from the fact that an IQ score can be significantly changed by even a small amount of well-directed practice, there are other arguments against these tests.

First, the Berkeley Study on Creativity showed that a person whose IQ assessment was high was not necessarily: independent in thought; independent in action; either possessed of or able to value a good sense of humour; appreciative of beauty; reasonable; relativistic; able to enjoy complexity and novelty; original;

comprehensively knowledgeable; fluent; flexible; or astute.

Secondly, those who argue that IQ does measure a wide and absolute range of human abilities have failed to consider that the test should be concerned with three major areas: 1) the brain being tested; 2) the test itself; 3) the results. Unfortunately the IQ protagonists have become too obsessed with the test and the results and have neglected the real nature of the brain being tested.

They have failed to realise that their tests do not test basic human ability, but measure untrained and undeveloped human performance. Their claims are much like those of an imaginary surveyor of women's feet sizes in the Orient at the time when their feet were restricted to make them small. From the crib the foot was placed in bandages until the woman was nearly full grown. This was done to stunt the growth and to produce 'dainty' feet.

To assume, however, as the surveyor might have done, that these measurements represent natural and fully developed bodily dimensions is as absurd as it is to assume that intelligence tests measure the natural dimensions of our minds. Our minds, like the women's feet, have been 'bound' by the way we have misjudged and mistrained them, and are therefore not naturally developed.

In defence of IQ tests, it is interesting to note their history. They were *not* developed as a method, so often assumed, of 'suppressing the masses'. On the contrary, the French psychologist Binet observed that those children getting higher education were almost exclusively from the upper classes. He considered this unfair, and devised the first IQ tests in order to allow *any* child with developed mental abilities to qualify for ongoing studies. The tests gave unparalleled opportunities for children who would otherwise have been deprived.

Consider IQ tests as games, or 'markers' of a current stage of mental development in a few specified areas. They can then be used both to gauge present developments in those areas, and as a basis from which those skills can be improved and developed, and the IQ score raised appropriately.

THE HUMAN BABY – A MODEL OF EXCELLENCE

Another most convincing case for the excellence of the human brain is the functioning and development of the human baby. Far from being the 'helpless and incapable little thing' that many people assume it to be, it is the most extraordinary learning, remembering and intellectually advanced being – even in its most early stages it surpasses the performance of the most sophisticated computers.

With very few exceptions, all babies learn to speak by the time they are two, and many even earlier. Because this is so universal it is taken for granted, but if the process is examined more closely it is seen to be extremely complex.

Try listening to someone speaking while pretending that you have no knowledge of language and very little knowledge of the objects and ideas the language discusses. Not only will this task be difficult, but because of the way sounds run into each other the distinction between different words will often be totally unclear. Every baby who has learned to talk has overcome not only these difficulties but also the difficulties of sorting out what makes sense and what doesn't. When he is confronted with sounds like 'koooochiekooo-chiekooooooooooaahhhhisn'tealovelelyli'ldarling!' one wonders how he ever manages to make sense of us at all!

The young child's ability to learn language involves him in processes which include a subtle control of, and an inherent understanding of, rhythm, mathematics, music, physics, linguistics, spatial relations, memory; integration, creativity, logical reasoning and thinking – left and right cortex working from the word go.

You who still doubt your own abilities have yourself learned to talk and to read. You should therefore find it difficult to attack a position of which you yourself are evidence for the defence.

There really is no doubt that your brain is capable of infinitely more complex tasks than has been thought. The remainder of *Use Your Head* will shed light on a number of the areas in which performance and self-realisation can be achieved.

Personal notes and applications

3 How the human brain has been reined in

OVERVIEW

▶ **Why performance does not match potential**

▶ **'Only human'!**

▶ **The operations manual for the brain**

WHY PERFORMANCE DOES NOT MATCH POTENTIAL

Even with the mounting evidence, a number of people still remain sceptical about the potential of the human brain, pointing to the performance of most of us as a contradiction of that evidence. In response to this objection a questionnaire was given to people from all areas of life to determine why this amazing organ is so under-used. The questions are noted below, and underneath each question is noted the reply given by at least 95 per cent. As you read ask yourself the questions.

▶ In school were you taught anything about your brain and how understanding its functions could help you learn, memorise, think, etc?
No.

▶ Were you taught anything about how your memory functions?
No.

▶ Were you taught anything about special and advanced memory techniques?
No.

▶ Anything about how your eye functions when you are learning and about how you can use this knowledge to your advantage?
No.

▶ Anything about the ranges of study techniques and how they can be applied to different disciplines?
No.
▶ Anything about the nature of concentration and how to maintain it when necessary?
No.
▶ Anything about motivation, how it affects your abilities, and how you can use it to your advantage?
No.
▶ Anything about the nature of key words and key concepts and how they relate to note taking and imagination etc?
No.
▶ Anything about thinking?
No.
▶ Anything about creativity?
No.

By now the answer to the original objection should be clear: the reasons why our performances do not match even our minimum potentials is that we are given no information about what we are, or about how we can best utilise our inherent capacities.

'ONLY HUMAN'!

Another survey I have carried out over the last thirty years, and in fifty different countries, is to ask people to imagine themselves in the following situation:

They have 'completed' an assignment, and the results are totally and utterly disastrous. They attempt to avoid taking responsibility, by giving such standard excuses for failure as 'so and so didn't send me the fax on time', 'I had to go to the doctor *just* at the crucial time in the project', 'It was *their* fault – if the communications systems in this company had been better, everything would have been all right', 'My boss wouldn't let me do it in the way I suggested', and so on.

They are next asked to imagine that despite all their brilliant excuse-making, they are finally 'cornered' and have to admit that the whole catastrophe was indeed their responsibility.

Finally, they are asked to complete the 'admission of guilt' sentence that people commonly use: 'All *right*, all *right*, it was my fault, but what do you expect, I'm . . . . !'

In every group surveyed, in every country, and in every language, the unanimous phrase to complete the sentence was: 'only human!'

Humorous though this may initially seem, it reflects a worldwide and seriously misguided myth that the human being is somehow fundamentally inadequate and flawed, and that it is *this* that is responsible for the mounting catalogue of human 'mistakes' and 'failures'.

To gain another perspective on the scenario described above, consider these opposites: you have done an astounding job, and people are beginning to call you 'extraordinary, wonderful, amazing, a genius, brilliant', and they are describing your work as 'astounding, the best they have ever seen, unbelievable, and unparalleled in its excellence'. For a little while you go through the standard routines of denial, but in the end have to admit to your excellence. How many times have you yourself or have you seen other people stand up proudly and pronounce 'Yes! I am brilliant, I am a genius, and the job I have done is indeed amazing – so amazing it amazed even me! and the reason is because *I'm human!*'

Probably never . . .

And yet it is this second scenario that is the more natural and indeed appropriate of the two. For the human being, you, as has been described in chapter 2, is indeed an extraordinary, and many would say miraculous creation.

The reason for our 'mistakes' and 'failures' is not that we are 'only human' but that at this very early stage in our evolution we are still taking our first, babyish and tentative steps towards an understanding of the astounding bio-computer we each possess.

The reason that in our worldwide educational systems we have spent so little time learning about how to learn is that we as a race have not known the fundamental principles of the operation of that bio-computer.

To use a modern computer metaphor, we have not known about the software for the hardware of the brain.

THE OPERATIONS MANUAL FOR THE BRAIN

Use Your Head is the first 'Operations Manual' designed to help you understand your own 'super-biocomputer', to nurture and care for it, and to unleash the natural and extraordinary range of mental skills you possess.

4 Reading faster and more efficiently

OVERVIEW

► **Reading problems**

► **Reading defined**

► **Why reading problems exist**

► **Reading eye movements**

► **Advantages of faster reading**

► **False beliefs about reading**

► **Advanced reading techniques – faster and faster**

► **Motivational practice**

► **Metronome training**

READING PROBLEMS

In the space below and over the page note *all* the problems you have with reading and learning. Be strict with yourself. The more you are able to define, the more completely you will be able to improve.

Note your own definition of the word *Reading*.

Reading teachers have noted over the past fifteen years that in each of their classes, the same general problems arise. Below is the list of those most commonly experienced. The reader is advised to check his own against these, adding to his own list any others that apply – there will probably be quite a few.

vision	fatigue	recall
speed	laziness	impatience
comprehension	boredom	vocabulary
time	interest	subvocalisation
amount	analysis	typography
surroundings	criticism	literary style
noting	motivation	selection
retention	appreciation	rejection
age	organisation	concentration
fear	regression	back-skipping

Each of the problems in the table above is serious, and can by itself disrupt reading and learning. This book is devoted to solving these problems, the current chapter being concerned primarily with vision, speed, comprehension, and the learning environment.

Before getting down to the more physical aspects of reading I shall first define the term, then in the light of this definition shall explain why the wide range of problems that exist is so universally experienced.

READING DEFINED

Reading, which is often defined as 'getting from the book what the author intended' or 'assimilating the written word' deserves a far more complete definition. It can be defined as follows: *Reading is the individual's total interrelationship with symbolic information. It is usually the visual aspect of learning, and contains the following seven steps*:

1 recognition
The reader's knowledge of the alphabetic symbols. This step takes place almost before the physical aspect of reading begins.

2 assimilation
The physical process by which light is reflected from the word and is received by the eye, then transmitted via the optic nerve to the brain. *See fig 7 (page 25).*

3 intra-integration
The equivalent to basic comprehension and refers to the linking of all parts of the information being read with all other appropriate parts.

4 extra-integration

This includes analysis, criticism, appreciation, selection and rejection. The process in which the reader brings the whole body of his previous knowledge to the new knowledge he is reading, making the appropriate connections.

5 retention

The basic storage of information. Storage can itself become a problem. Most readers will have experienced entering an examination room and storing most of their information during the two hour exam period! Storage, then, is not enough in itself, and must be accompanied by recall.

6 recall

The ability to get back out of storage that which is needed, preferably *when* it is needed.

7 communication

The use to which the information is immediately or eventually put; includes the very important subdivision: thinking.

The definition includes consideration of many of the problems listed on page 37. The only problems not included are those which are, in a sense, 'outside' the reading process, such as the influence of our reaction to our surroundings, time of day, energy level, interest, motivation, age and wellness.

WHY READING PROBLEMS EXIST

You may justifiably ask at this point why so many people experience the problems noted.

The answer, in addition to our previous lack of knowledge about the brain, lies in our approach to the initial teaching of reading. Most of you reading this book who are over twenty-five will probably have been taught by the Phonic or Alphabet Method. Others will probably have been taught by either this or by the Look and Say Method.

The most simplified Phonic Method teaches the child first the alphabet, then the different sounds for each of the letters in the alphabet, then the blending of sounds in syllables, and finally the blending of sounds forming words. From this point on he is given progressively more difficult books, usually in the form of series graded 1 to 10, through which he progresses at his own speed. He becomes a 'silent' reader during the process.

The Look and Say Methods teach children by presenting them with cards on which there are pictures. The names of the objects shown are clearly printed underneath them. Once a child has become familiar with the pictures and the names associated with them, the pictures are removed leaving only the words. When the child has built up enough basic vocabulary he progresses through a series of graded books similar to those for the child taught by the Phonic Method, and also becomes a 'silent' reader.

The outlines given of the two methods are necessarily brief, and there are at least fifty other methods similar to these presently being taught in England and in other English-speaking countries. Similar problems exist all over the world.

The point about these methods, however, is not that they are inadequate for achieving their aim, but that they are inadequate for teaching any child to read in the complete sense of the word.

Referring to the definition of Reading, it can be seen that these methods are designed to cover only the stage of recognition in the process, with some attempt at assimilation and intra-integration. The methods do not touch on the problems of speed, time, amount, retention, recall, selection, rejection, note-taking, concentration, appreciation, criticism, analyses, organisation, motivation, interest, boredom, surroundings, fatigue or typographic style, etc.

It can thus be seen that there is justification for the problems so widely experienced.

Recognition, it is important to note, is hardly ever mentioned as a problem, because it has been taught separately in the early years of school. All the other problems are mentioned because they have *not* been dealt with during the educational process.

Later chapters deal with the majority of these problems. The remainder of this chapter is devoted to eye movement, comprehension and the speed of your reading.

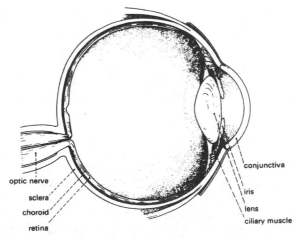

optic nerve

sclera

choroid

retina

conjunctiva

iris

lens

ciliary muscle

Fig 9 Your eye.

READING EYE MOVEMENTS

When asked to show with their forefingers the movement and speed of their eyes as they read most people move their fingers along in smooth lines from left to right, with a quick jump from the end of one line back to the beginning of the next. They normally take between a quarter to one second for each line.

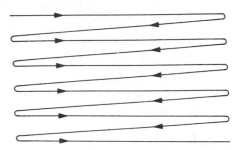

Fig 10 Assumed reading eye movement as shown by people with no knowledge of eye movements. Each line is thought to be covered in less than one second. *See text this page.*

Two major errors are being made.

Speed
Even if the eye moved as slowly as one line per second, words would be covered at the rate of 600–700 words per minute (wpm). As the average reading speed on even light material is 240 wpm, it can be seen that even those estimating slower speeds assume that they cover words much more rapidly than they really do.

Movement
If eyes moved over print in the smooth manner shown above they would be able to take in nothing, because the eye can see things clearly only when it can 'hold them still'. If an object is still, the eye must be still in order to see it, and if an object is moving, the eye must move with the object in order to see it. A simple experiment either by yourself or with a friend will confirm this: hold a forefinger motionless in front of the eyes and either feel your own eyes or watch your friend's eyes as they look at the object. They will remain still. Next move the finger up, down, sideways and around, following it with the eyes. And finally move the finger up, down and around, holding the eyes still, or cross both hands in front of your face, at the same time looking at them both simultaneously. (If you can accomplish this last feat write to me immediately!) When objects move, eyes move with them if they are to be seen clearly.

Relating all this to reading, it is obvious that if the eyes are going to take in words, and if the words are still, the eyes will have to pause on each word before moving on. Rather than moving in smooth lines as shown in fig 10 (opposite), the eyes in fact move in a series of stops and quick jumps.

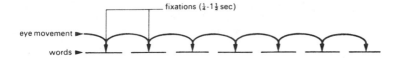

Fig 11 Diagram representing the stop-and-start movement of the eyes during the reading process. *See text this page.*

The jumps themselves are so quick as to take almost no time, but the fixations can take anywhere from ¼ to 1½ seconds. A person who normally reads one word at a time – and who skips back over words and letters is forced, by the simple mathematics of his eye movements, into reading speeds which are often well below 100 wpm, and which mean that he will not be able to understand much of what he reads, nor be able to read much.

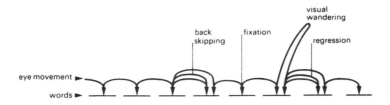

Fig 12 Diagram showing poor reading habits of slow reader: one word read at a time, with unconscious back-skipping, visual wandering, and conscious regressions. *See text this page.*

It might seem at first glance that the slow reader is doomed, but the problem can be solved, and in more than one way.

Speeding up

1 Skipping back over words can be eliminated, as 90 per cent of back-skipping and regression is based on apprehension and is unnecessary for understanding. The 10 per cent of words that do

need to be reconsidered can be noted in Mind Map form as outlined in Chapters 7 and 8 or can be intelligently guessed, marked and looked up later.

2 The time for each fixation can be reduced to approach the ¼ second minimum – the reader need not fear that this is too short a time, for his eye is able to register as many as five words in one one-hundredth of a second.

3 The size of the fixation can be expanded to take in as many as three to five words at a time.

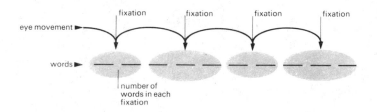

Fig 13 Diagram showing eye movements of a better and more efficient reader. More words are taken in at each fixation, and back-skipping, regression and visual wandering are reduced.

This solution might at first seem impossible if it is true that the mind deals with one word at a time. In fact it can equally well fixate in *groups* of words, which is better in nearly all ways: When we read a sentence we do not read it for the individual meaning of each word, but for the meaning of the phrases in which the words are contained.

Reading for example, the   cat
          sat   on   the
road is more difficult than reading the cat sat   on the road.

The slower reader has to do more mental work than the faster, smoother reader because he has to add the meaning of each word to the meaning of each following word. In the above example this amounts to five or six additions. The more efficient reader, absorbing in meaningful units, has only one simple addition.

ADVANTAGES OF FASTER READING

An advantage for the faster reader is that his eyes will be doing less physical work on each page. Rather than having as many as 500 fixations tightly focused per page as does the slow reader, he will have as few as 100 fixations per page, each one of which is less muscularly fatiguing.

Another advantage is that the rhythm and flow of the faster reader will carry him comfortably through the meaning, whereas the slow reader, because of his stopping and starting, jerky approach, will be far more likely to become bored, to lose concentration, to mentally drift away and to lose the meaning of what he is reading.

FALSE BELIEFS ABOUT READING

It can be seen from this that a number of commonly held beliefs about faster readers are false:

Words must be read one at a time:
Wrong. Because of our ability to fixate and because we read for meaning rather than for single words.

Reading faster than 500 wpm is impossible:
Wrong. Because the fact that we can take in as many as six words per fixation and the fact that we can make four fixations a second means that speeds of 1,000 wpm are perfectly feasible.

The faster reader is not able to appreciate:
Wrong. Because the faster reader will be understanding more of the meaning of what he reads, will be concentrating on the material more, and will have considerably more time to go back over areas of special interest and importance to him.

Higher speeds give lower concentration:
Wrong. Because the faster we go the more impetus we gather and the more we concentrate.

Average reading speeds are natural and therefore the best:
Wrong. Because average reading speeds are not natural. They are speeds produced by an incomplete initial training in reading, combined with an inadequate knowledge of how the eye and brain work at the various speeds possible.

ADVANCED READING TECHNIQUES – FASTER AND FASTER

Apart from the general advice given above, some readers may be able to benefit from the following information which is usually prac-tised in conjunction with a qualified instructor:

Visual aid techniques:
When children learn how to read they often point with their finger to the words they are reading. We have traditionally regarded this as a fault and have told them to take their fingers off the page. It is now

realised that it is we and not the children who are at fault. Instead of insisting that they remove their fingers we should ask them to move their fingers faster. It is obvious that the hand does not slow down the eye, and the added values that the aid gives in establishing a smooth rhythmical habit are immeasurable.

To observe the difference between unaided and aided eye movement, ask a friend to imagine a large circle about one foot in front of him, and then ask him to look slowly and carefully around the circumference. Rather than moving in a perfect circle, his eyes will follow a pattern more resembling an arthritic rectangle.

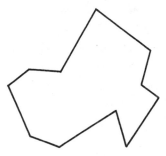

Fig 14 Pattern showing unaided eye movement attempting to move around the circumference of a circle. *See text this page.*

Next trace a circle in the air with your finger asking your friend to follow the tip of your finger as you move smoothly around the circumference. You will observe that the eyes will follow almost perfectly and will trace a circle similar to that shown below.

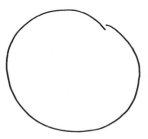

Fig 15 Pattern showing aided eye movement around the circumference of a circle. *See text this page.*

This simple experiment also indicates what an enormous improvement in performance there can be if a person is given the basic information about the physical function of the eye and brain. In many instances no long training or arduous practising is necessary. The results, as in this case, are immediate.

The reader is not restricted to the use of his forefinger as a visual aid, and can use to advantage a pen or a pencil, as many naturally efficient readers do. At first the visual aid will make the reading speed look slow. This is because, as mentioned earlier, we all imagine that we read a lot faster than we actually do. But the aided reading speed will actually be faster.

Expanded focus
In conjunction with visual aid techniques, the reader can practise taking in more than one line at a time. This is certainly not physically impossible and is especially useful on light material or for overviewing and previewing. It will also improve normal reading speeds. It is very important always to use a visual guide during this kind of reading, as without it the eye will tend to wander with comparatively little direction over the page. Various patterns of visual aiding should be experimented with, including diagonal, curving, and straight-down-the-page movements.

High speed perception
This exercise involves turning pages as fast as possible, attempting to see as many words per page as possible. This form of training will increase the ability to take in large groups of words per fixation, will be applicable to overviewing and previewing techniques, and will condition the mind to much more rapid and efficient general reading practices. This high speed conditioning can be compared to driving along a motorway at 90 miles an hour for one hour. Imagine you had been driving at this speed, and you suddenly came to a road sign saying 'slow to 30'. To what speed would you slow down if somebody covered your speedometer and said 'go on, tell me when you reach 30'. The answer of course would be 50 to 60 mph.

The reason for this is that the mind has become conditioned to a much higher speed, which becomes 'normal'. Previous 'normals' are more or less forgotten in the presence of the new ones. The same applies to reading, and after a high speed practice you will often find yourself reading at twice the speed without even feeling the difference. *See fig 16 (overleaf)*.

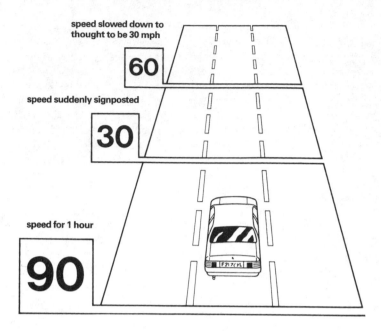

speed slowed down to
thought to be 30 mph

60

speed suddenly signposted

30

speed for 1 hour

90

Fig 16 Illustrations showing how the mind 'gets used to' speed and motion. The same kind of relativistic 'misjudgments' can be used to advantage to help us learn to learn more adequately. *See text on page 45.*

MOTIVATIONAL PRACTICE

Most reading is done at a relaxed and almost lackadaisical pace, a fact of which many speed reading courses have taken advantage. Students are given various exercises and tasks, and it is suggested to them that after each exercise their speed will increase by 10–20 wpm. And so it does, often by as much as 100 per cent over the duration of the lessons. The increase, however, is often due not to the exercises, but to the fact that the student's motivation has been eked out bit by bit during the course.

The same significant increases could be produced by guaranteeing each student, at the beginning of the course, the fulfilment of any wish he desired. Performance would immediately equal those normally achieved at the end of such courses – similar to the unathletic fellow who runs 100 metres in 10 seconds flat and jumps a 6-foot fence when being chased by a bull. In these cases motivation is the major factor, and the reader will benefit enormously by consciously applying it to each learning experience. If a deep-rooted decision is made to do better, then poor performance will automatically improve.

The graph on the following page is provided for readers wishing to chart their speed reading progress. To calculate your speed in words per minute, take the following steps:

1 Read for one minute – note start and stopping points.

2 Count the number of words on three lines.

3 Divide that number by three to give you the average number of words per line.

4 Count the total number of lines read (balancing short lines out).

5 Multiply the average number of words per line by the number of lines you read, which will equal your reading speed in words per minute (wpm).

NB The formula for working out speed in wpm is:

$$\text{wpm (speed)} = \frac{\text{number of pages read} \times \text{number of words per average page}}{\text{number of minutes spent reading}}$$

METRONOME TRAINING

A metronome, which is usually used for keeping musical rhythm, can be most useful for both reading and high speed reading practices. If you set it at a reasonable pace, each beat can indicate a single sweep for your visual aid. In this way a steady and smooth rhythm can be maintained and the usual slowdown that occurs after a little while can be avoided. Once the most comfortable rhythm has been found, your reading speed can be improved by occasionally adding an extra beat per minute.

The metronome can also be used to pace the high speed perception exercises, starting at slower rates and accelerating to exceptionally fast rates, 'looking' at one page per beat.

The information on eye movements, visual aids and advanced reading techniques should be applied by the reader to each of his reading situations. It will be found that these techniques and items of advice will become more useful when applied together with information and techniques from other chapters.

For those especially interested in pursuing the full range of speed and range reading skills, refer to my book *Speed (and Range) Reading* (see page 151).

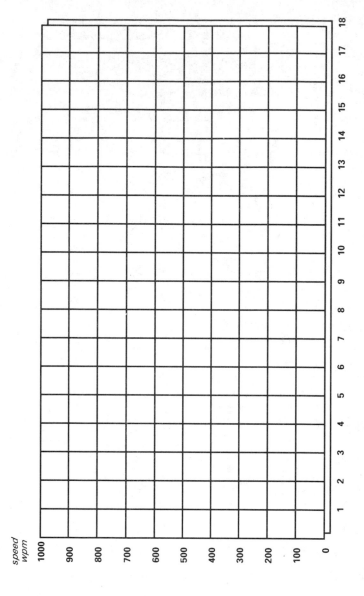

See text on page 47.

Personal notes and applications

5 Memory

OVERVIEW

QUESTIONS ON MEMORY

Test 1 Recall *during* learning

On the next page is a list of words. Read each word on this list once, quickly, in order, and then turn to page 56 and fill in as many of the words as you can. You may not be able to remember all of them, so simply try for as many as possible. Read the complete list, one after the other. To ensure you do this properly use a small card, covering each word as you read it.

start now

went
the
book
work
and
good
and
start
of
the
late
white
and
paper
Leonardo da Vinci
light
of
skill
the
own
stair
note
and
rode
will
time
home

Now turn to page 56 and answer questions 1–6.

Test 2 Recall *during* learning

At the top of page 58 is a blank graph. Fill it in with a line which repre-sents the amount you think your memory recalls **during** a learning period. The vertical left-hand line marks the **starting point** for the learning; the vertical right-hand line marks the point when **learning stops**; the bottom line represents no recall at all (complete for-getting); and the top line represents perfect recall.

On pages 53 and 54 are examples of graphs filled in by three people, representing the amount they felt their memories recalled **during** a learning period. These graphs start at 75% because it is assumed that most standard learning does not produce 100% understanding or recall. There are, of course, many other alternatives, so when you have looked at these, turn to page 58 and complete the graph for the way you think *your* recall works.

Fig 17 Three example of graphs indicate recall during a learning period.

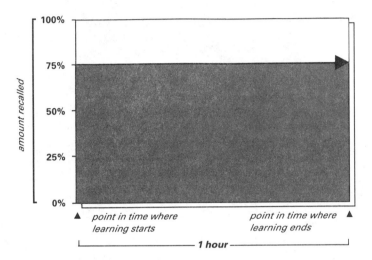

A who thought his recall stayed constant during his learning.

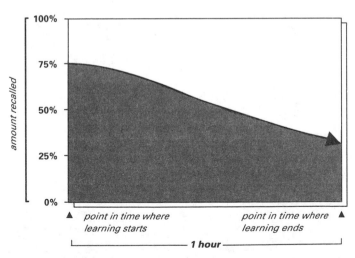

B who thought he remembered more from the beginning of a learning period and less from the end.

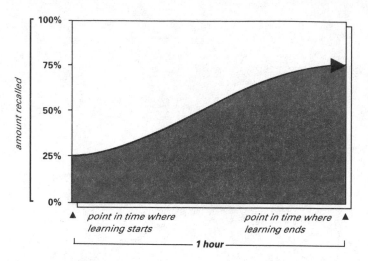

C who thought he remembered less from the start and more from the end.

Test 3 Recall *after* learning

At the bottom of page 58 is a blank graph to show the way your memory behaves **after** a learning period has been completed. The vertical left-hand line marks the end point of your learning; there is no right-hand vertical line because it is assumed that the 'afterwards' would be for a few years!; the bottom line represents no recall at all; and the top line represents perfect recall. These graphs show three people's assessment of their recall after learning.

Fig 18 Graphs filled in to show recall after a learning period has been completed.

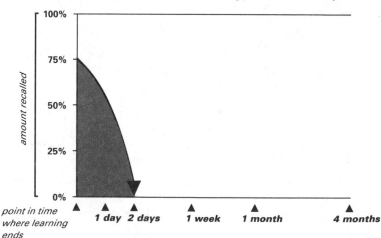

A who thought he forgot nearly everything in a very short period of time.

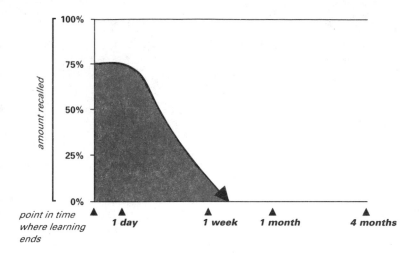

B who thought his recall was constant for a little while and then dropped off fairly steeply.

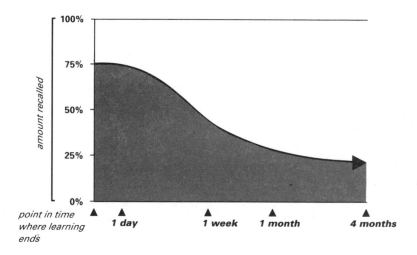

C who thought his memory stayed constant for a while and then dropped off more slowly, levelling out at a certain point.

As with Test 2 there are many alternatives, so now turn to page 58 and complete the graph in the way which most closely represents what you feel to be your normal pattern of forgetting. For the purpose of the exercise you can assume that nothing happens after your learning period to remind you of the information you learned.

TEST RESPONSES AND FURTHER QUESTIONS

Test 1: responses   Recall *during* learning

When answering the questions, do not refer to the original list

1 Fill in as many of the words, in order, as you can.

2 How many of the words from the beginning of the list did you remember before making the first error?

3 Can you recall any words which appeared more than once in the list? If so note them.

4 How many of the words within the last five did you remember?

5 Do you remember any item from the list which was outstandingly different from the rest?

6 How many words from the middle of the list can you remember which you have not already noted in answers to previous questions?

Test 2: responses   Recall *during* learning

Fill in, as demonstrated in the examples of fig 17 (*pages 53–54*), the line which represents the way your memory recalls **during** a learning period.

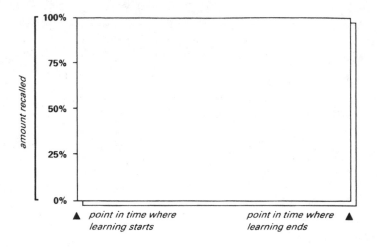

Test 3: responses   Recall *after* learning

Fill in the graph below in the way you think your recall behaves **after** a learning period has been completed. *See examples fig 18 (pages 54–55).*

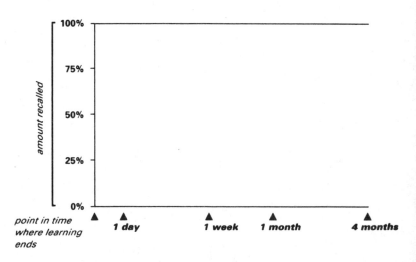

RECALL *DURING* LEARNING –
DISCUSSION OF TESTS 1 AND 2

Test 1 showed how recall functions **during** a period of learning, as long as understanding remains fairly constant (the words in the list were not 'difficult').

In this test virtually everyone has the following results: anywhere between 2 and 8 of the words at the beginning of the list are recalled; most of the words which appear more than once are recalled (in this case 'the', 'and', 'of'); one or two of the last five words are recalled; and the outstanding word or phrase is recalled (in this case Mohammed Ali); very few of the words from the middle are recalled.

This is a pattern of test scores which shows very dramatically that **memory** and **understanding** do not work in exactly the same way as time progresses – all the words were understood, but only some were recalled. The differences between the way in which memory and understanding function help explain why so many people find they don't recall very much after hours of learning and understanding. The reason is that recall tends to get progressively worse as time goes on unless the mind is given brief rests. *See fig 19 (below).*

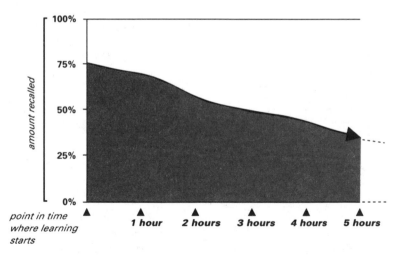

Fig 19 As time goes on, recall of material being learned tends to get progressively worse unless the mind is given proper rests. *See text this page.*

Thus the graph requested in Test 2 will be more complex than the simple examples given. It will probably also be more complex than the graph you have traced for your own recall behaviour during learning. Average scores from Test 1 produce a graph similar to fig 20 (*below*).

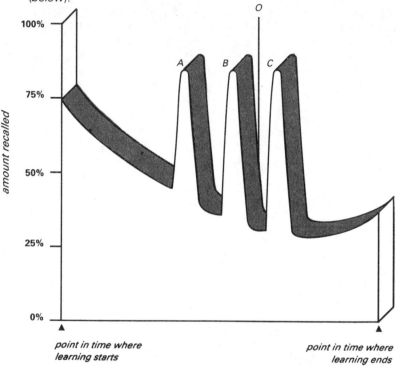

Fig 20 Recall **during** learning. Graph indicating that we recall more from the beginning and ends of a learning period. We also recall more when things are associated or linked (A, B and C) and more when things are outstanding or unique (O). *See text pages 59, 60 and 61.*

From the graph it is clear that under normal circumstances and with understanding fairly constant, we tend to recall: more at the beginning and ends of learning periods; more of items which are associated by repetition, sense, rhyming etc.; more of things which are outstanding or unique (the psychologist who discovered this characteristic was Von Restorff, and such a memorisation event is known as the Von Restorff effect); and considerably *less* of things from the middle of learning periods.

If recall is going to be kept at a reasonable level, it is necessary to find the point at which recall and understanding work in greatest harmony. For normal purposes this point occurs in a time period of between 20 to 50 minutes. A shorter period does not give the mind enough time to appreciate the rhythm and organisation of the material, and a longer period results in the continuing decline of the amount recalled (*as graphed in fig 19, page 59*).

If a period of learning from a lecture, a book or the mass media is to take two hours, it is far better to arrange for brief breaks during these two hours. In this way the recall curve can be kept high, and can be prevented from dropping during the later stages of learning. The small breaks will guarantee eight relatively high points of recall, with four small drops in the middle. Each of the drops will be less than the main drop would have been were there no breaks. *See fig 21 (below).*

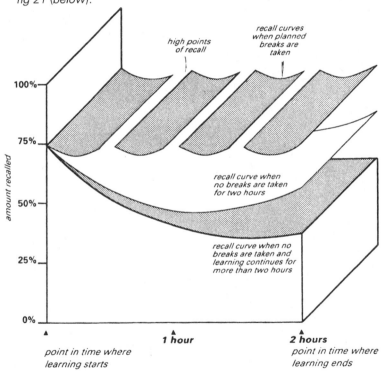

Fig 21 Recall **during** learning – with and without breaks. A learning period of between 20–50 minutes produces the best relationship between understanding and recall. *See text this page.*

Breaks are additionally useful as relaxation points. They get rid of the muscular and mental tension which inevitably builds up during periods of concentration.

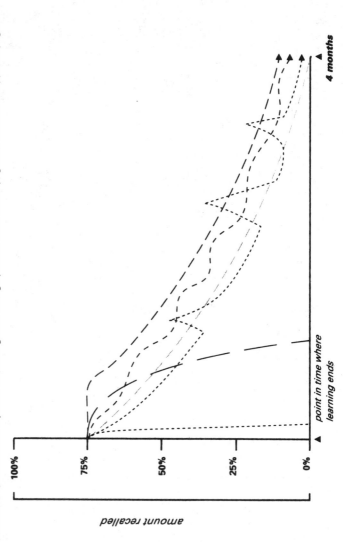

Fig 22 Recall *after* a learning period – people's estimates. Graph showing the different kinds of answers people gave when asked to show how their recall functioned after a period of learning. Add YOUR graph here from Test 3 (page 54). *See text on opposite page.*

RECALL *AFTER* LEARNING –
DISCUSSION OF TEST 3 AND ANSWERS

In Test 3 you were asked to fill in a graph indicating the way you thought your recall functioned after a period of learning had been completed. The examples on pages 54 and 55 were answers many people have given when asked this question, although a much wider variety of responses overall was registered.

Apart from those graphed on pages 54 and 55, other answers included: straight lines plunging almost immediately to nothing: variations on the more rapid drop, some falling to 0%, others always maintaining some per cent, however small; variations on the slower fall-off, also with some falling to 0% and others maintaining; and variations on these themes, showing rises and falls of varying degree. *See fig 22 opposite.*

The surprising truth of the matter is that none of the examples shown earlier, and none of the estimates shown, is correct. They

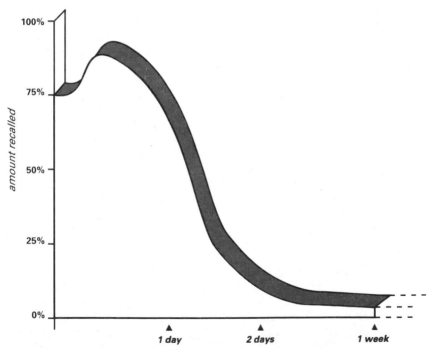

Fig 23 Graph showing how human recall rises for a short while after learning, and then falls steeply (80% of detail forgotten within 24 hours). *See text pages 63 and 64.*

have all neglected a particularly significant factor: recall after a learning period initially *rises*, and only then declines, following a steeply falling concave curve that levels off. *See fig 23 (page 63).*

Once it is realised that the brief rise does take place, the reason for it can be understood: at the very moment when a learning period is finished, the brain has not had enough time to integrate the new information it has assimilated, especially the last items. It needs a few minutes to complete and link firmly all the interconnections within the new material – to let it 'sink in'.

The decline that takes place after the small rise is a steep one – within 24 hours of a one-hour learning period at least 80 per cent of detailed information is lost. This enormous drop must be prevented, and can be by proper techniques of Mind Mapping and review.

MEMORY – REVIEW TECHNIQUES AND THEORY

If review is organised properly, the graph shown in fig 23 can be changed to keep recall at the high point reached shortly after learning has been completed. In order to accomplish this, a programmed pattern of review must take place, each review being done at the time just before recall is about to drop. For example, the first review should take place about 10 minutes after a one-hour learning period and should itself take 5 minutes. This will keep the recall high for approximately one day, when the next review should take place, this time for a period of 2 to 4 minutes. After this, recall will probably be retained for approximately a week, when another 2 minutes review can be completed followed by a further review after about one month. After this time the knowledge will be lodged in Long Term Memory. This means it will be familiar in the way a personal telephone number is familiar, needing only the most occasional nudge to maintain it. *See fig 24 (opposite).*

The first review, especially if notes have been taken, should be a fairly complete note revision which may mean scrapping original notes and substituting for them revised and final copy. The second, third and fourth etc. review sessions should take the following form: without referring to final notes, jot down on a piece of paper everything that can be recalled. This should then be checked against the final notes and any corrections or additions to what has been recalled should be made. Both notes and jottings should be in the form of Mind Maps, as explained on pages 93–101.

One of the most significant aspects of proper review is the accumulative effect it has on all aspects of learning, thinking and remem-

Fig 24 opposite Graph showing how properly spaced review can keep recall constantly high. *See text above.*

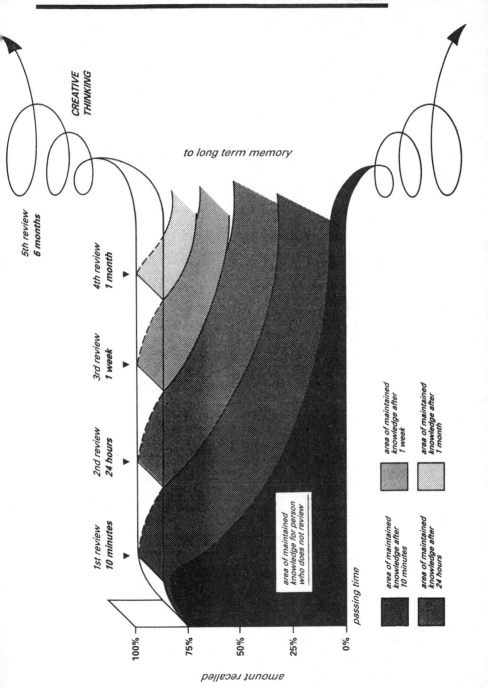

CREATIVE THINKING

5th review
6 months

to long term memory

4th review
1 month

3rd review
1 week

2nd review
24 hours

1st review
10 minutes

area of maintained
knowledge for person
who does not review

passing time

100%

75%

50%

25%

0%

amount recalled

area of maintained
knowledge after
10 minutes

area of maintained
knowledge after
24 hours

area of maintained
knowledge after
1 week

area of maintained
knowledge after
1 month

bering. The person who does not review is continually wasting the effort he does put in to any learning task, and putting himself at a serious disadvantage.

Each time he approaches a new learning situation his recall of previous knowledge gained will be at a very low ebb, and the connections which should be made automatically will be dismissed. This will mean that his understanding of the new material will not be as complete as it could be, and that his efficiency and speed through the new material will also be less. This continuingly negative process results in a downward spiral that ends in a general despair of ever being able to learn anything – each time new material is learned it is forgotten, and each time new material is approached it seems to become more oppressive. The result is that many people, after having finished their formal exams, seldom, if ever, approach text books again.

Failure to review is equally as bad for general memory. If each new piece of information is neglected, it will not remain at a conscious level, and will not be available to form new memory connections. As memory is a process which is based on linking and association, the fewer items there are in the 'recall store', the less will be the possibility for new items to be registered and connected.

On the opposite side of this coin, the advantages of reviewing are enormous. The more you maintain your current body of knowledge, the more you will be able to absorb and handle. When you study, the expanding amount of knowledge at your command will enable you to digest new knowledge far more easily, each new piece of information being absorbed in the context of your existing store of relevant information, see fig 24 (page 65). The process is much more like that of the traditional snowball rolling, where the snowball gets rapidly bigger the more it rolls and eventually continues rolling under its own momentum. This will enhance your confidence, your work and your life.

SPECIAL MEMORY SYSTEMS AND MNEMONICS

Test 4 Memory Systems

Here is a list of words next to numbers. As with Test 1 read each item once, covering the ones read with a card as you progress down the list. The purpose of this is to remember which words went with which number:

4 leaf
9 shirt
1 table
6 orange
10 poker
5 student
8 pencil
3 cat
7 car
2 feather

Now turn over and fill in the answers in the order requested.

Test 4: responses   Memory Systems

Here are the numbers 1 to 10. From memory, fill in next to each number the word which originally appeared next to it. The numbers are not listed in the same order as before. Refer back after you have filled in as many as you can.

1	7
5	4
3	6
8	10
9	2

Score _____

The Systems

Since the time of the Greeks certain individuals have impressed their fellow men with the most amazing feats of memory. They have been able to remember hundreds of items backwards and forwards and in any order; dates and numbers; names and faces; and have been able to perform special memory feats such as memorising whole areas of knowledge perfectly, or remembering decks of cards in the order anyone chose to present them.

In most cases these individuals were using special Memorising Principles known as mnemonics. Traditionally these Principles have been scorned as mere tricks, but recently the attitude towards them has changed. It has been realised that the methods which initially enable minds to remember something more easily and quickly, and then to remember it for much longer afterwards, actually use the brain's natural ability.

Current knowledge about the ways in which our minds work shows that these principles are indeed closely connected to the basic ways in which the brain functions. The use of Mnemonic Principles has consequently gained respectability and popularity, and they are currently being taught in universities and schools as additional aids in the general learning process. The improvement of memory performances that can be achieved is quite remarkable, and the range of techniques is wide.

Indeed, the beginning of the 1990s saw the establishment of The Memoriad, the World Memory Championships. As a result of these championships, staggering feats of memory are being achieved, previous psychological limits are being smashed, the boundaries of what is possible are being extended and amazing new records established. Dominic O'Brien, the first World Memory Champion, has already memorised a complete pack of cards in 42.6 seconds, as well as memorising a randomly generated 100-digit binary number in 57 seconds! For more information on the possibilities of memory and mental world records, see *Use Your Memory* and *Buzan's Book of Genius*.

There is not enough space in the present chapter to give a complete coverage, but I shall introduce in the next few pages the basic theory behind the system, and a simple system for remembering up to ten items.

Assuming that the items to be remembered are:

1 **table**
2 **feather**
3 **cat**
4 **leaf**
5 **student**
6 **orange**
7 **car**
8 **pencil**
9 **shirt**
10 **poker**

In order to remember these it is necessary to have some system which enables us to use the **associative** and **linking** power of memory to connect them with their proper number.

The best system for this is the Number-Rhyme System, in which each number has a rhyming word connected to it.

The rhyming key words are:

1 **bun**
2 **shoe**
3 **tree**
4 **door**
5 **hive**
6 **sticks**
7 **heaven**
8 **skate**
9 **vine**
10 **hen**

In order to remember the first list of arbitrary words it is necessary to link them in some strong manner with the rhyming words connected to the numbers. If this is done successfully, the answer to a question such as 'what word was connected to number 3?' will be easy. The rhyming word for 5, 'hive', will be recalled automatically and with it will come the connected image of the word that has to be remembered. *See Colour Plate I.*

'SMASHIN' SCOPE' OF MEMORY

The important thing in this and all other memory systems is to make sure that the rhyming word and the word to be remembered are totally and securely linked together. In order to do this, the connecting images must be one or many of the following:

1 Synaesthesia/sensuality

Synaesthesia refers to the blending of the senses. The great 'natural' memorisers, and the great mnemonists, developed exceptional sensitivity in each of their senses, and then blended these senses to produce enhanced recall. In developing the memory it has been found to be essential to sensitise increasingly and train regularly your senses of:

a) vision
b) hearing
c) smell
d) taste
e) touch
f) kinaesthesia – your awareness of bodily position and movement in space.

2 Movement/motivation

In any mnemonic image, movement adds another giant range of possibilities for your brain to 'link in' and thus remember. As your images move, make them three-dimensional.

3 Association

Whatever you wish to memorise, make sure you associate or link it to something stable in your mental environment, i.e. Peg system: one = bun.

4 Sexuality

We all have a virtually perfect memory in this area. Use it!

5 Humour

Have fun with your memory. The more funny, ridiculous, absurd and surreal you make your images, the more outstandingly memorable they will be. Salvador Dali, the surrealist painter, said that, 'My paintings are photographs painted by hand of the irrational made concrete' and that in many instances they are the paintings of the perfectly held memories of his day and night dreams.

6 Imagination

Einstein said, 'Imagination is more important than knowledge. For knowledge is limited, whereas imagination embraces the entire world, stimulating progress, giving birth to evolution.' The more you apply your imagination to memory, the better your memory will be.

7 Number

Numbering adds specificity and efficiency to the principle of order and sequence.

8 Symbolism

Substituting a more meaningful image for a more normal or boring image increases the probability of recall. You may also use traditional symbols, e.g. stop sign or light bulb.

9 Colour

Where appropriate, and whenever possible, use the full range of the rainbow, to make your ideas more 'colourful' and therefore more memorable.

10 Order and/or sequence

In combination with the other principles, order and/or sequence allows for much more immediate reference, and increases the brain's possibilities for 'random access'. Expanded use of order and sequence allows you to develop Memory Matrices, such as the Self-Enhancing Memory Matrix, enabling you to memorise as many as 10,000 items of information and more (see *Master Your Memory*).

11 Positivity

In most instances positive and pleasant images are better for memory purposes, because they make the brain *want* to return to the images. Certain negative images, even though applying all the principles above, and though in and of themselves 'memorable', could be blocked by the brain because it finds the prospect of returning to such images unpleasant.

12 Exaggeration

In all your images, exaggerate size, shape, and sound.

These can easily be remembered by the mnemonic anagram **smashin' scope**.

THE NUMBER-RHYME SYSTEM

It is important, when forming the images, to have a very clear mental picture in front of your inner eye. To achieve this it is often best to close your eyes and to project the image on to the inside of your eyelid, or on to a screen inside your head, and to hear, feel, smell or experience it in the way that works best for you. (For example, think of what you ate for lunch yesterday: how does your brain recreate it for you? Use the same medium.)

To make all this clearer, let us try the ten items given.

1 bun   table

Imagine a giant bun on top of a fragile table which is in the process of crumbling from the weight. Smell the fresh cooked aroma, taste your favourite bun.

2 shoe   feather

Imagine your favourite shoe with an enormous feather growing out of the inside, preventing you from putting your shoe on, tickling and tickling your feet.

3 tree   cat

Imagine a large tree with either your own cat or a cat you know stuck in the very top branches frantically scrambling about and mewing loudly.

4 door   leaf

Imagine your bedroom door as one giant leaf, crunching and rustling as you open it.

5 hive   student

Imagine a student at his desk, dressed in black and yellow stripes, buzzing busily, or with honey dripping on his pages.

6 sticks   orange

Imagine large sticks puncturing the juicy surface of an orange that is as big as a beach ball. Feel and smell the juice of the orange squirting out.

7 heaven   car

Imagine all the angels sitting on cars rather than clouds; experience yourself driving the car you consider heavenly.

8 skate   pencil

Imagine yourself skating over the pavement, hearing the sound of the wheels on the ground, as you see the multi-coloured pencils attached to your skates creating fantastic art wherever you go.

9 vine   shirt

Imagine a vine as large as Jack and the Bean Stalk's bean stalk, and instead of leaves on the vine, hang it all over with brightly coloured shirts blowing in the wind.

10 hen   poker

Have fun!

Now fill in as many of the words as you can on the next page.

With a little practice it would be possible to remember ten out of ten each time, even though using the same system. The words to be remembered can, like the clothes they were compared to, be taken off the hook and other clothes substituted. The words which must remain constant and which in any case are almost impossible to forget are the rhyming key words.

As mentioned earlier there are many other systems which are equally as easy to remember as this simple one but would take (and already have done) another book to explain. Ones which are particularly useful include the Major System, which enables recall of more than a thousand items in the manner of the Number-Rhyme System, as well as giving a key for memorising numbers and dates, and the Face-Name System which helps prevent the embarrassing and wide-spread habit of not being able to recall either the names or faces of people you have met. For further information on these Systems, see *Use Your Memory* and *Master Your Memory*.

THE 'IMPOSSIBLE' TASK

As you will have gathered throughout the development of this chapter, memory is primarily an associative and linking process which depends in large part on **Key Words** and key concepts properly imagined. These memory/mnemonic techniques really *do* work – sometimes so well as to be considered by some unbelievable. A class of fourteen-year-old students in Sweden were set, by their teacher, what he described as an impossible task, stating that they should simply try to do as well as they could. The class was, in one evening, to memorise as many of the countries and capitals of the world as they could.

One of the children was a young boy who went home particularly oppressed and depressed by the task, and told his father of what he thought was an unfair assignment. His father had taken a Use Your Head Course, and enthusiastically set about teaching his son how to apply memory techniques to what was in reality not that difficult at all.

Two weeks later the father was phoned by the headmaster of the school, apologising for having to convey the bad news that his son had been cheating. Upon questioning by the father, the headmaster explained that in a recent geography test, the top mark in the school had been 123, and that his son had scored over 300, 'proving' that he had cheated!

The story ended happily, with the boy in question teaching his schoolmates how to use *their* memories.

Although the chapter entitled Memory is coming to an end the next three chapters on Mind Mapping are themselves very closely connected with remembering and recalling. The information in this chapter should be reviewed after the following chapters have been completed.

As a final *review*, check your improving memory once again. In the spaces below write the rhyming key word for the Number-Rhyme System, and next to it the words used earlier in the chapter to illustrate the system.

Rhyming key words   **word connected**

1 _____   _____

2 _____   _____

3 _____   _____

4 _____   _____

5 _____   _____

6 _____   _____

7 _____   _____

8 _____   _____

9 _____   _____

10 _____   _____

Personal notes and applications

6 Mind Maps® – an introduction to the nature of words and thought

OVERVIEW

▶ **Exercise and discussion – Kusa-Hibari**

▶ **Key Words – Recall and Creative**

▶ **Multi-ordinate nature of words**

▶ **Key Word versus standard notes**

EXERCISE AND DISCUSSION

Imagine that your hobby is reading short stories, that you read at least five a day, and that you keep notes so that you will not forget any of them. Imagine also that in order to ensure a proper recall of each story you use a card filing system. For each story you have one card for the title and author, and a card for every paragraph. On each of these paragraph cards you enter a main and a secondary key word or phrase. The key words/phrases you take either directly from the story or make up yourself because they summarise particularly well.

Imagine further that your ten thousandth story is *Kusa-Hibari* by Lafcadio Hearne, and that you have prepared the title-and-author card.

Now read the story on pages 78–80, and for the purpose of this exercise enter a key recall word or phrase for both the main and secondary idea for the first five paragraphs only, in the space provided on page 80.

KUSA-HIBARI
Lafcadio Hearne

1 His cage is exactly two Japanese inches high and one inch and a half wide: its tiny wooden door, turning upon a pivot, will scarcely admit the tip of my little finger. But he has plenty of room in that cage – room to walk, and jump, and fly, for he is so small that you must look very carefully through the brown-gauze sides of it in order to catch a glimpse of him. I have always to turn the cage round and round, several times, in a good light, before I can discover his whereabouts, and then I usually find him resting in one of the upper corners – clinging, upside down, to his ceiling of gauze.

2 Imagine a cricket about the size of an ordinary mosquito – with a pair of antennae much longer than his own body, and so fine that you can distinguish them only against the light. Kusa-Hibari, or 'Grass-Lark' is the Japanese name of him; and he is worth in the market exactly twelve cents: that is to say, very much more than his weight in gold. Twelve cents for such a gnat-like thing! . . . By day he sleeps or meditates, except while occupied with the slice of fresh egg-plant* or cucumber which must be poked into his cage every morning . . . to keep him clean and well fed is somewhat trouble-some: could you see him, you would think it absurd to take any pains for the sake of a creature so ridiculously small.

3 But always at sunset the infinitesimal soul of him awakens: then the room begins to fill with a delicate and ghostly music of indescri-bable sweetness – a thin, silvery rippling and trilling as of tiniest electric bells. As the darkness deepens, the sound becomes sweeter – sometimes swelling till the whole house seems to vibrate with the elfish resonance – sometimes thinning down into the faintest imaginable thread of a voice. But loud or low, it keeps a penetrating quality that is weird . . . All night the atom thus sings: he ceases only when the temple bell proclaims the hour of dawn.

4 Now this tiny song is a song of love – vague love of the unseen and unknown. It is quite impossible that he should ever have seen or known, in this present existence of his. Not even his ancestors, for many generations back, could have known anything of the night-life of the fields, or the amorous value of song.

5 They were born of eggs hatched in a jar of clay, in the shop of some insect-merchant: and they dwelt thereafter only in cages. But he sings the song of his race as it was sung a myriad years ago, and as faultlessly as if he understood the exact significance of every note. Of course he did not learn the song. It is a song of organic memory – deep, dim memory of other quintillions of lives, when the ghost of him shrilled at night from the dewy grasses of the hills.

---

* aubergine

Then that song brought him love – and death. He has forgotten all about death: but he remembers the love. And therefore he sings now – for the bride that will never come.

6 So that his longing is unconsciously retrospective: he cries to the dust of the past – he calls to the silence and the gods for the return of time . . . Human lovers do very much the same thing without knowing it. They call their illusion an Ideal: and their Ideal is, after all, a mere shadowing of race-experience, a phantom of organic memory. The living present has very little to do with it. . . . Perhaps his atom also has an ideal, or at least the rudiment of an ideal; but, in any event, the tiny desire must utter its plaint in vain.

7 The fault is not altogether mine. I had been warned that if the creature were mated, he would cease to sing and would speedily die. But, night after night, the plaintive, sweet, unanswered trilling touched me like a reproach – became at last an obsession, an affliction, a torment of conscience; and I tried to buy a female. It was too late in the season; there were no more kusa-hibari for sale, – either males or females. The insect-merchant laughed and said, 'He ought to have died about the twentieth day of the ninth month.' (It was already the second day of the ten month.) But the insect-merchant did not know that I have a good stove in my study, and keep the temperature at above 75°F. Wherefore my grass-lark still sings at the close of the eleventh month, and I hope to keep him alive until the Period of Greatest Cold. However, the rest of his generation are probably dead: neither for love nor money could I now find him a mate. And were I to set him free in order that he might make the search for himself, he could not possibly live through a single night, even if fortunate enough to escape by day the multitude of his natural enemies in the garden – ants, centipedes, and ghastly earth-spiders.

8 Last evening – the twenty-ninth of the eleventh month – an odd feeling came to me as I sat at my desk: a sense of emptiness in the room. Then I became aware that my grass-lark was silent, contrary to his wont. I went to the silent cage, and found him lying dead beside a dried-up lump of egg-plant as grey and hard as a stone. Evidently he had not been fed for three or four days; but only the night before his death he had been singing wonderfully – so that I foolishly imagined him to be more than usually contented. My student, Aki, who loves insects, used to feed him; but Aki had gone into the country for a week's holiday, and the duty of caring for the grass-lark had developed upon Hana, the housemaid. She is not sympathetic, Hana the housemaid. She says that she did not forget the mite – but there was no more egg-plant. And she had never thought of substituting a slice of onion or of cucumber! . . . I spoke words of reproof to Hana the housemaid and she dutifully expressed contrition. But

the fairy-music had stopped: and the stillness reproaches; and the room is cold, in spite of the stove.

9 Absurd! . . . I have made a good girl unhappy because of an insect half the size of a barley-grain! The quenching of that infinitesimal life troubled me more than I could have believed possible. . . . Of course, the mere habit of thinking about a creature's wants – even the wants of a cricket – may create, by insensible degrees, an imaginative interest, an attachment of which one becomes conscious only when the relation is broken. Besides, I had felt so much, in the hush of the night, the charm of the delicate voice – telling of one minute existence dependent upon my will and selfish pleasure, as upon the favour of a god – telling me also that the atom of ghost in the tiny cage, and the atom of ghost within myself, were forever but one and the same in the deeps of the Vast of being. . . . And then to think of the little creature hungering and thirsting, night after night and day after day, while the thoughts of his guardian deity were turned to the weaving of dreams! . . . How bravely, nevertheless, he sang on to the very end – an atrocious end, for he had eaten his own legs! . . . May the gods forgive us all – especially Hana the housemaid!

10 Yet, after all, to devour one's own legs for hunger is not the worst that can happen to a being cursed with the gift of song. There are human crickets who must eat their own hearts in order to sing.

Key words or phrases for main and secondary ideas from *Kusa-Hibari*

	main	secondary
paragraph 1	_____	_____
paragraph 2	_____	_____
paragraph 3	_____	_____
paragraph 4	_____	_____
paragraph 5	_____	_____

Opposite you will find sample key words and phrases from the notes of students who have previously done this exercise. Briefly compare and contrast these with your own ideas.

Students' suggested key words and phrases

	main	**secondary**
paragraph 1	his cage	two Japanese inches
	wooden door	wooden floor
	ceiling of gauze	plenty of room
	small insect	discover whereabouts
paragraph 2	cricket	Grass-Lark
	weight in gold	twelve cents
	antennae	market
	Kusa-Hibari	gnatlike
paragraph 3	sleep	fresh cucumber
	clean and well fed	pains
	occupied	meditation
	absurd	small
paragraph 4	penetrating	silvery rippling
	music	house vibrating
	electric bells	penetrating
	soul	hour of dawn
paragraph 5	love	night-life
	amorous	insect merchant
	the hills	significance
	death	love and death

In class situations instructors then circled one word from each section:

	main	**secondary**
paragraph 1	wooden door	discover whereabouts
2	weight in gold	market
3	occupied	pains
4	penetrating	hour of dawn
5	love	night-life

Students were then asked to explain why, in the context of the exercise, these words and phrases and not others had been selected. Answers usually included the following: 'good image words', 'imaginative', 'descriptive', 'appropriate', 'good for remembering', 'evocative', etc.

Only one student in fifty realised why the instructors had chosen these words: in the context of the exercise the series chosen was disastrous.

To understand why, it is necessary to imagine a time some years after the story has been read when you are going to look at the notes again for recall purposes. Imagine that some friends have played a prank, taking out the title cards of some of your stories and challenging you to remember the titles and authors. You would have no idea to start with to which story your cards referred, and would have to rely solely on them to give you back the correct images.

With the Key Words at the bottom of page 81, you would probably be forced to link them in the following way: 'wooden ˷or', a general phrase, would gain a mystery-story air when you read 'discover whereabouts'. The next two keys 'weight in gold' and 'marke˄' would confirm this, adding a further touch of intrigue suggesting a criminal activity. The next three key words, 'occupied', 'pains' and 'penetrating' might lead you to assume that one of the characters, perhaps the hero, was personally in difficulty, adding further tension to the ongoing plot as the 'hour of dawn', obviously an important and suspense-filled moment in the story, approached. The final two keys, 'love' and 'night-life' would add a romantic or risqué touch to the whole affair, encouraging you to thumb quickly through the remaining key words in search of further adventures and climaxes! You would have created an interesting new story, but would not remember the original one.

Words which seemed quite good at the time have not, for some reason, proved adequate for recall. To explain why, it is necessary to discuss the difference between Key Recall Words and Key Creative Words, and the way in which they interact after a period of time has passed. Good recall words would have been the following:

	main	secondary
paragraph 1	cage	2 Japanese inches
2	cricket	Grass-lark
3	sleep	fresh cucumber
4	music	amorous value
5	song	organic memory

Understanding why these words are better for recall can be based on the way in which we realise the human brain processes information.

KEY WORDS – RECALL AND CREATIVE

A Key Recall Word or phrase is one which funnels into itself a wide range of special images, and which, when it is triggered, funnels back the same images. It will tend to be a strong noun or verb, on occasion being surrounded by additional Key adjectives or adverbs. *See fig 25 (opposite).*

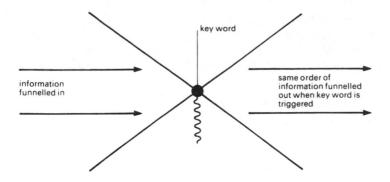

Fig 25 Diagram representing Key Recall Word. *See text on opposite page.*

A Creative Word is one which is particularly evocative and image-forming, but which is far more general than the more directed Key Recall Word. Words like 'ooze' and 'bizarre' are especially evocative but do not necessarily bring back a specific image. *See fig 26 (below).*

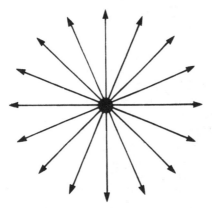

Fig 26 A Key Creative Word sprays out associations in all directions. *See text this page.*

Apart from understanding the difference between Creative and Recall Words, it is also necessary to understand the nature of words themselves as well as the nature of the brain which uses them.

MULTI-ORDINATE NATURE OF WORDS

Every word is 'multi-ordinate', which simply means that each word is like a little centre on which there are many, many little hooks. Each hook can attach to other words to give both words in the new pair slightly different meanings. For example the word 'run' can be hooked quite differently in 'run like hell' and 'her stocking has a run in it'. *See Colour Plate II.*

In addition to the multi-ordinate nature of words, each brain is also different from each other brain. As shown in the first chapter, the number of connections a brain can make within itself is almost limitless. Each individual also experiences a very different life from each other individual (even if two people are enjoying the 'same experience' together they are in very different worlds: A is enjoying the experience with B as a major part of it, and B is enjoying the experience with A as a major part of it). Similarly the associations that each person will have for any word will be different from everybody else's. Even a simple word like 'leaf' will produce a different series of images for each person who reads or hears it. A person whose favourite colour is green might imagine the general greenness of leaves; someone whose favourite colour is brown, the beauty of autumn; a person who had been injured falling out of a tree, the feeling of fear; a gardener, the different emotions connected with the pleasure of seeing leaves grow and the thought of having to rake them all up when they had fallen, etc. One could go on for ever and still not satisfy the range of associations that you who are reading this book might have when *you* think of leaves.

As well as the unique way in which the mind sees its personal images, each brain is also, by nature, both creative and sense-organising. It will tend to 'tell itself interesting and entertaining stories' as it does for example when we day- or night-dream.

The reason for the failure of the recall and general words selected from *Kusa-Hibari* can now clearly be seen. When each of the multi-ordinate words or phrases was approached, the mind automatically picked the connecting hooks which were most obvious, most image-producing, or the most sense-making. The mind was consequently led down a path that was more creative than recall based, and a story was constructed that was interesting, but hardly useful for remembering. *See Plate II centre.*

Key Recall Words would have forced the mind to make the proper links in the right direction, enabling it to recreate the story even if for all other intentional purposes it had been forgotten. *See Plate II bottom.*

KEY WORD VERSUS STANDARD NOTES

The main body of a person's recalling is of this Key concept nature. It is not, as is often assumed, a word-for-word verbatim process. When people describe books they have read or places they have been to, they do not start to 're-read' from memory. They give Key concept overviews outlining the main characters, settings, events and add descriptive detail. Similarly the single Key word or phrase will bring back whole ranges of experience and sensation. Think for example of the range of images that enter your mind when you read the word 'child'.

How, then, does acceptance of these facts about Key Recall affect our attitude towards the structure of note taking?

Because we have become so used to speaking and writing words, we have mistakenly assumed that normal sentence structure is the best way to remember verbal images and ideas. Thus the majority of students and even graduates have taken notes in a normal literary fashion similar to the example of a university student whose notes were rated 'good' by his professor. *See next page.*

Our new knowledge of Key concepts and recall has shown that in this type of notes 90 per cent of the words are not necessary for recall purpose. This frighteningly high figure becomes even more frightening when a closer look is taken at what happens with standard sentence notes:

1 Time is wasted recording words which have no bearing on memory (estimated waste – 90%).

2 Time is wasted re-reading the same unnecessary words (estimated waste – 90%).

3 Time is wasted searching for the words which *are* Key Recall Words, for they are usually not distinguished by any marks and thus blend in with othe non-recall words.

4 The connections between Key Recall Words are interrupted by words that separate them. We know that memory works by association and any interference by non-recall words will make the connections less strong.

5 The Key Recall Words are separated in time by intervening words: after one Key word or phrase has been read it will take at least a few seconds to get to the next. The longer the time between connections, the less chance there will be of proper connection being made.

6 The Key Recall Words are separated in space by their distance from each other on the page. As with the point made about time,

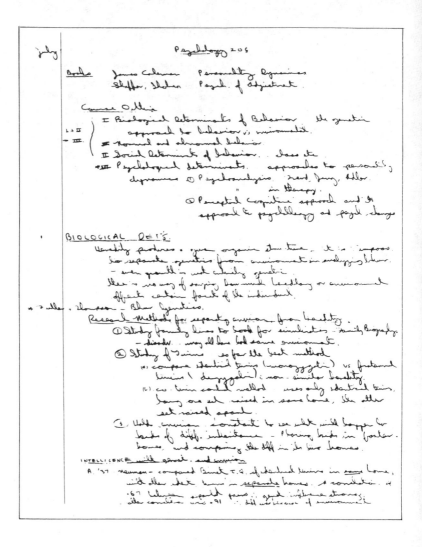

Fig 27 An example of a student's traditionally 'good' university notes. *See text on previous page.*

the greater the distance between the words, the less chance of there being a proper connection.

You are advised to practise Key Recall Word and phrase selection from any previous notes made during periods of study. It will also be helpful at this point for you to summarise this chapter in Key note form.

In addition, reconsider Key Recall and creative words in the light of the information in the chapter on Memory, especially the section dealing with Mnemonic Principles. Similarly the memory chapter itself can be reconsidered in the light of this chapter, with a similar emphasis on the relationship and similarities between Mnemonic systems and Key and creative concepts.

The review graph is another important consideration. Review is made much easier when notes are in Key form, because less time is expended, and because the recall itself will be superior and more complete. Any weak linkages will also be cemented more firmly in the early stages.

Finally, linkages between Key Recall words and concepts should always be emphasised and where possible simple lists and lines of Key words should be avoided. In the following chapter advanced methods of Key Recall Word linking and patterning will be explained in full, in the technique called Mind Mapping.

Personal notes and applications

7 Mind Maps® – the natural laws

OVERVIEW

► **Exercise – space travel**

► **Linear history of speech and print**

► **Your brain and Mind Mapping**

► **Mind Mapping laws**

EXERCISE – SPACE TRAVEL

Prepare a half-hour speech on the topic of Space Travel on a separate piece of paper starting immediately after having reached the end of this paragraph. Allow no more than five minutes for the task, whether or not you have finished. This exercise will be referred to later in the chapter. Also any problems with thought organisation experienced in performing the task should be noted here.

Problems experienced

LINEAR HISTORY OF SPEECH AND PRINT

For the last few hundred years it has been popularly thought that man's mind worked in a linear or list-like manner. This belief was held primarily because of the increasing reliance on our two main methods of communication, speech and print.

In speech we are restricted, by the nature of time and space, to speaking and hearing one word at a time. Speech was thus seen as a linear or line-like process between people. *See fig 28* (*below*).

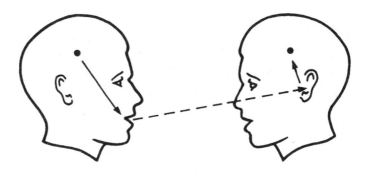

Fig 28 Speech has traditionally been seen as a list-like affair. *See text this page.*

Print was seen as even more linear. Not only was the individual forced to take in units of print in consecutive order, but print was laid out on the page in a series of lines or rows.

This linear emphasis overflowed into normal writing or notetaking procedures. Virtually everyone was (and still is) trained in school to take notes in sentences or vertical lists. (Most readers will probably have prepared their half-hour speech in one of these two ways, as shown in fig 29, opposite.) The acceptance of this way of thinking is so long-standing that little has been done to contradict it. However, recent evidence shows the brain to be far more multi-dimensional and pattern making, suggesting that in the speech/print arguments there must be fundamental flaws.

The argument which says that the brain functions linearly because of the speech patterns it has evolved fails to consider, as do the supporters of the absolute nature of IQ tests, the nature of the organism. It is easy to point out that when words travel from one

A Normal line structure – sentence-based

B Standard list structure – order-of-importance-based

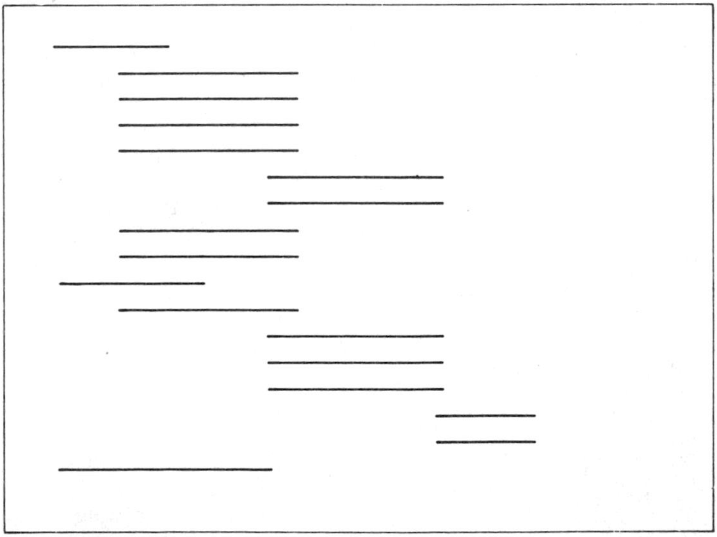

Fig 29 Standard forms of 'good' or 'neat' notes.

person to another they necessarily do so in a line, but this is not really the point. More to the point is the question: How does the brain which is speaking, and the brain which is receiving the words, deal with them *internally*?

The answer is that the brain is most certainly *not* dealing with them in simple lists and lines. You can verify this by thinking of the way in which your own thought processes work while you are speaking to someone else. You will observe that although a single line of words is coming out, a continuing and enormously complex process of sorting and selecting is taking place in your mind throughout the conversation. Whole networks of words and ideas are being juggled and interlinked in order to communicate a certain meaning to the listener.

Similarly the listener is not simply observing a long list of words like someone sucking up spaghetti. He is receiving each word in the context of the words that surround it. At the same time he is also giving the multi-ordinate nature of each word his own special interpretation as dictated by the structure of his personal information patterns and will be analysing, coding and criticising throughout the process.

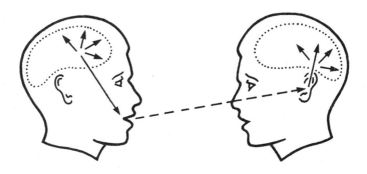

Fig 30 It is the network inside the mind, and not the simple order of word presentation, which is more important to an understanding of the way we relate to words. *See text pages 90–92.*

You may have noticed people suddenly reacting negatively to words you liked or thought were harmless. They react this way because the associations they have for these words are different from yours. Knowing this will help you understand more clearly the nature of conversations, disagreements and misunderstandings.

The argument for print is also weak. Despite the fact that we are trained to read units of information one after each other, that these are presented in lines and that we therefore write and note in lines, such linear presentation is not necessary for understanding, and in many instances is a disadvantage.

Your mind is perfectly capable of taking in information which is non-linear. In its day-to-day life it does this nearly all the time, observing all those things which surround it which include common *non*-linear forms of print: photographs, illustration, diagrams, etc. It is only our society's enormous reliance on linear information which has obscured the issue.

Your brain's non-linear character is further confirmed by recent biochemical, physiological and psychological research. Each area of research is discovering to its amazement and restrained delight that the brain is not only non-linear but is so complex and interlinked that it guarantees centuries of exhilarating research and exploration.

YOUR BRAIN AND MIND MAPPING

If the brain is to relate to information most efficiently the information must be structured in such a way as to 'slot in' as easily as possible. It follows that if the brain works primarily with Key concepts in an interlinked and integrated manner, our notes and our word relations should in many instances be structured in this way rather than in traditional 'lines'.

Rather than starting from the top and working down in sentences or lists, one should start from the centre with the main idea and branch out as dictated by the individual ideas and general form of the central theme.

A Mind Map such as that outlined in fig 31 (*overleaf*) has a number of advantages over the linear form of note taking.

1 The centre with the main idea is more clearly defined.

2 The relative importance of each idea is clearly indicated. More important ideas will be nearer the centre and less important ideas will be near the edge.

3 The links between the Key concepts will be immediately recognisable because of their proximity and connection.

4 As a result of the above, recall and review will be both more effective and more rapid.

5 The nature of the structure allows for the easy addition of new information without messy scratching out or squeezing in, etc.

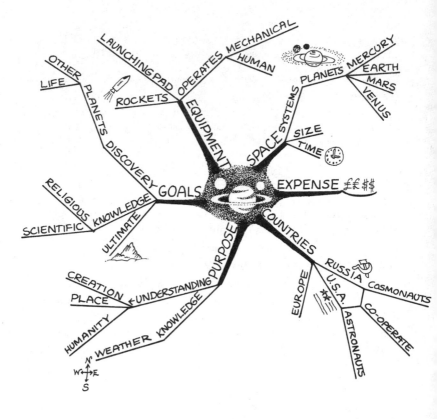

Fig 31 Initial ideas Mind Mapped around a central theme. *See text pages 93–95.*

6 Each map made will look and be different from each other map. This will aid recall.

7 In the more creative areas of note making, such as essay preparations etc, the open-ended nature of the map will enable the brain to make new connections far more readily.

In connection with these points, and especially with the last one, you should now do an exercise similar to your space travel speech at the beginning of this chapter, but this time using a Mind Map rather than the more linear methods. Follow the Mind Map laws given opposite.

MIND MAPPING LAWS

1 **Start with a coloured image in the centre.** An image often is 'worth a thousand words' and encourages creative thought while significantly increasing memory. Place the paper in a landscape position.

2 **Images throughout your Mind Map.** As No 1 and to stimulate all cortical processes, attract the eye and aid memory.

3 **Words should be printed.** For reading-back purposes a printed word gives a more photographic, clear, legible and more comprehensive feed-back. The little extra time that it takes to print is amply made up for in the time saved when reading back.

4 **The printed words should be on lines,** and **each line should be connected to other lines.** This is to guarantee that the Mind Map has basic structure.

5 Words should be in 'units', i.e. **one word per line.** This leaves each word more free hooks and gives note taking more freedom and flexibility.

6 Use **colours** throughout the Mind Map as they enhance memory, delight the eye and stimulate the right cortical process.

7 In creative efforts of this nature **the mind should be left as 'free' as possible.** Any 'thinking' about where things should go or whether they should be included will simply slow down the process.

　　The idea is to recall everything your mind thinks of around the central idea. As your mind will generate ideas faster than you can write, there should be almost no pause – if you do pause you will probably notice your pen or pencil dithering over the page. The moment you notice this get it back down and carry on. Do not worry about order or organisation as this will in many cases take care of itself. If it does not, a final ordering can be completed at the end of the exercise.

The Mind Mapping as thus described can be seen to eliminate all of the disadvantages of standard note-taking as outlined on page 85.

　　Use the Mind-Mapping laws above and the space provided on page 96 to branch out in the manner indicated in figure 31 (*opposite*) in a Mind Map preparation for a speech on 'Myself'.

　　Start the exercise now.

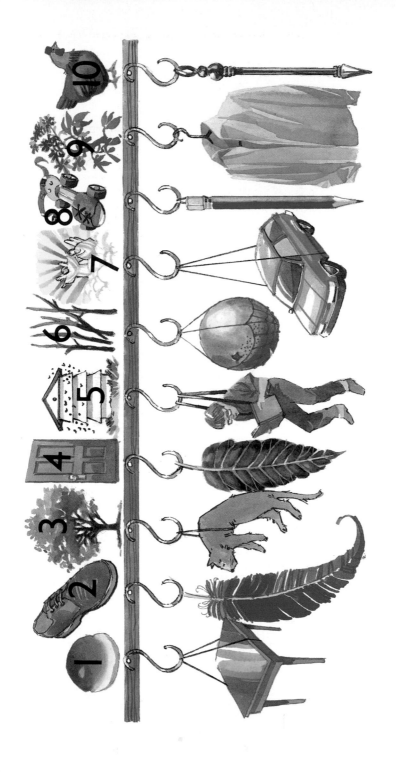

Plate I The Number Rhyme memory system. *See pages 70 to 73.*

Plate II top Each word is multi-ordinate, which means that it has a large number of 'hooks'. Each hook, when it attaches to another word, changes the meaning of the word. Think, for example, of how the meaning of the word 'run' changes in different contexts. *See page 84.*

Centre Because words are multi-ordinate, the mind can easily follow the wrong connections, especially with creative words. *See pages 82 to 84.*

Bottom When proper Key Recall Words are used the mind will make the right connections. *See pages 82 to 84.*

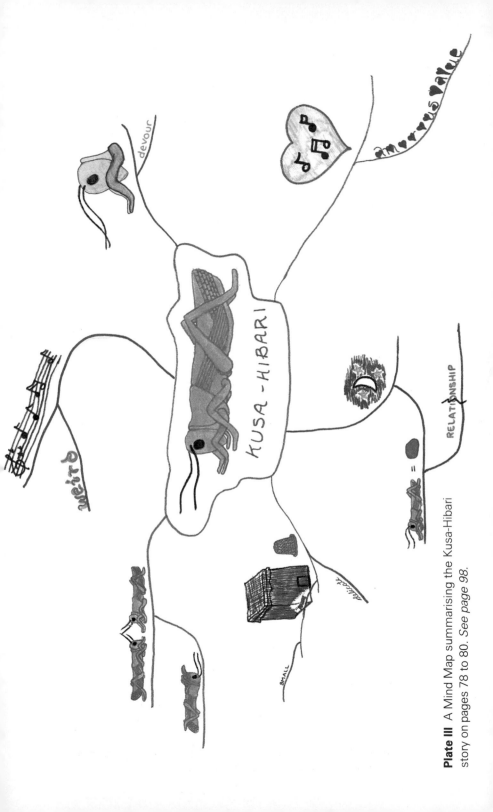

Plate III A Mind Map summarising the Kusa-Hibari story on pages 78 to 80. *See page 98.*

Plate IV Mind Map of Chapter 2. *See pages 93 to 102.*

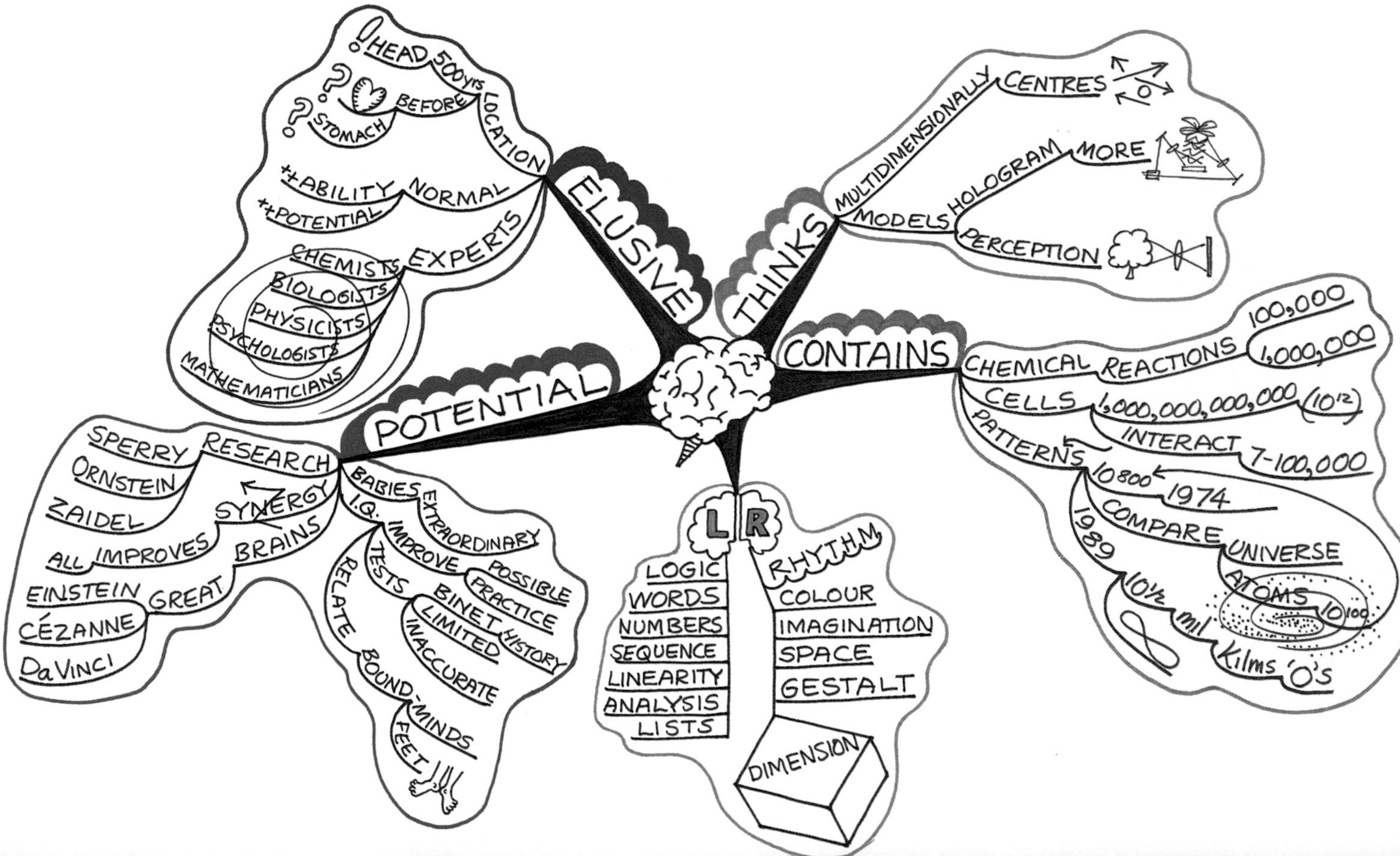

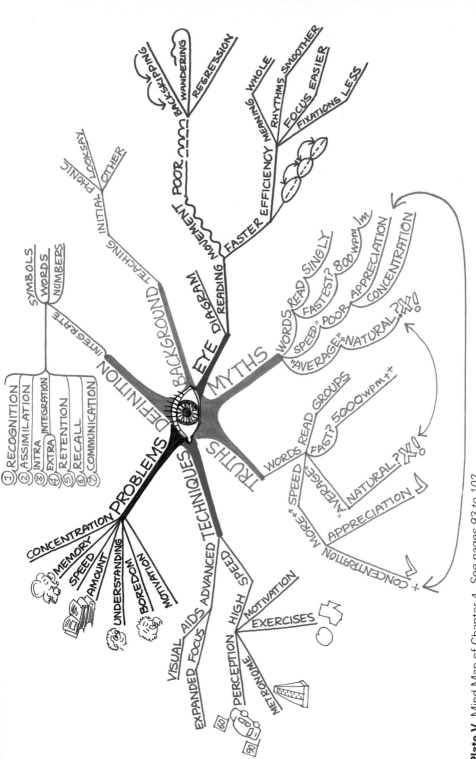

Plate V Mind Map of Chapter 4. *See pages 93 to 102.*

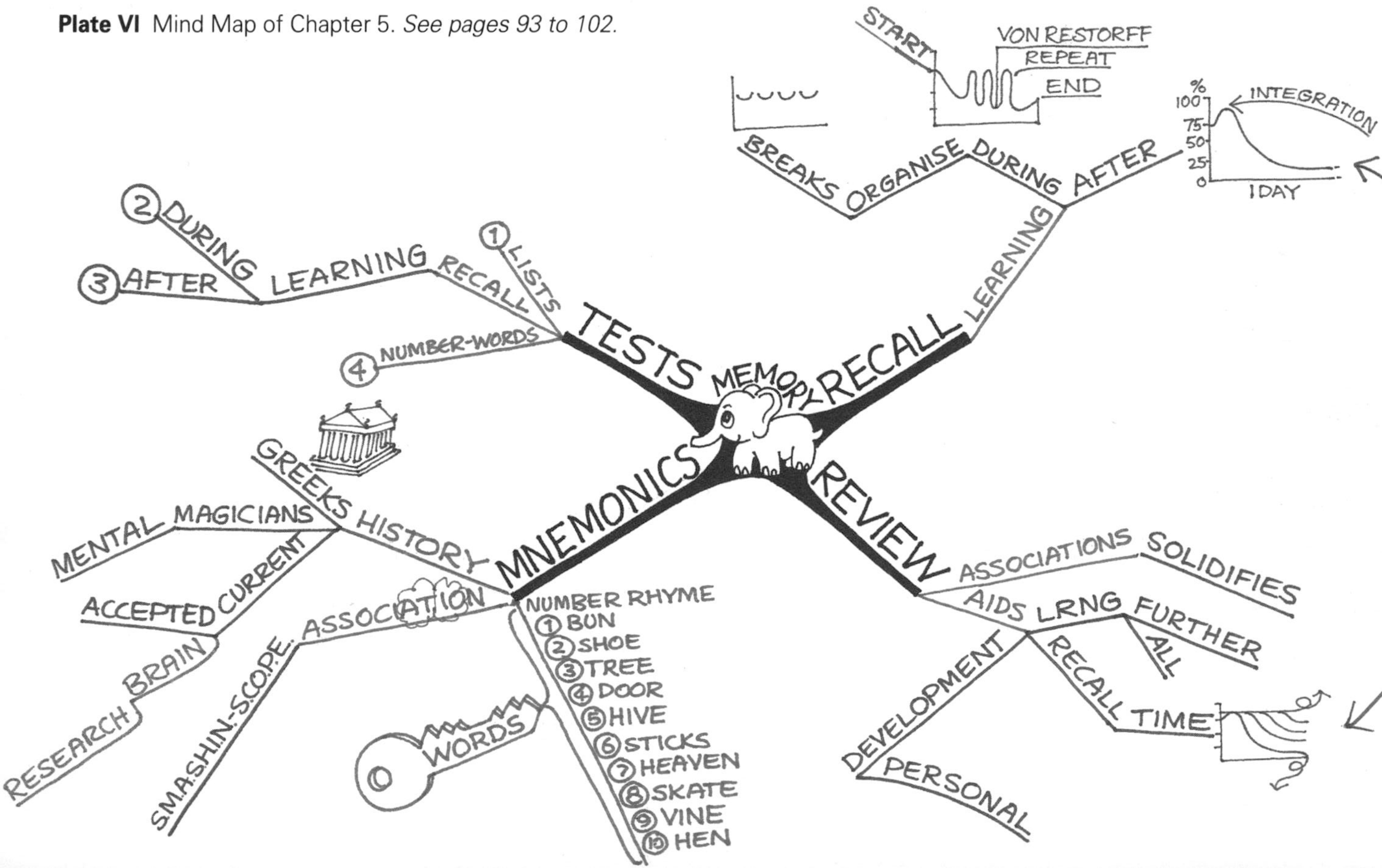

Plate VI Mind Map of Chapter 5. See pages 93 to 102.

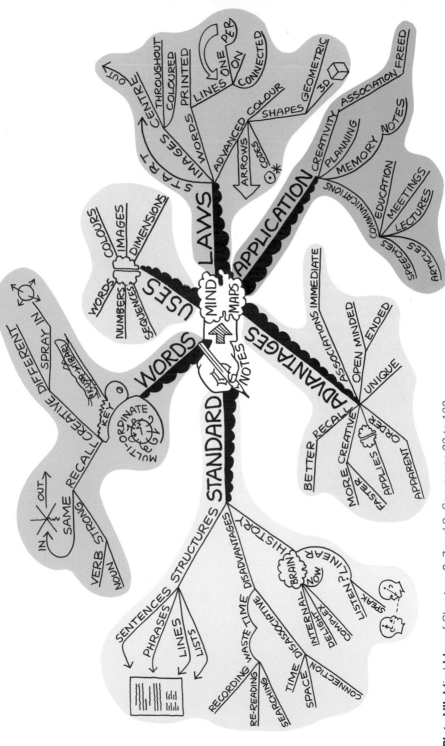

Plate VII Mind Map of Chapters 6, 7 and 8. See pages 93 to 102.

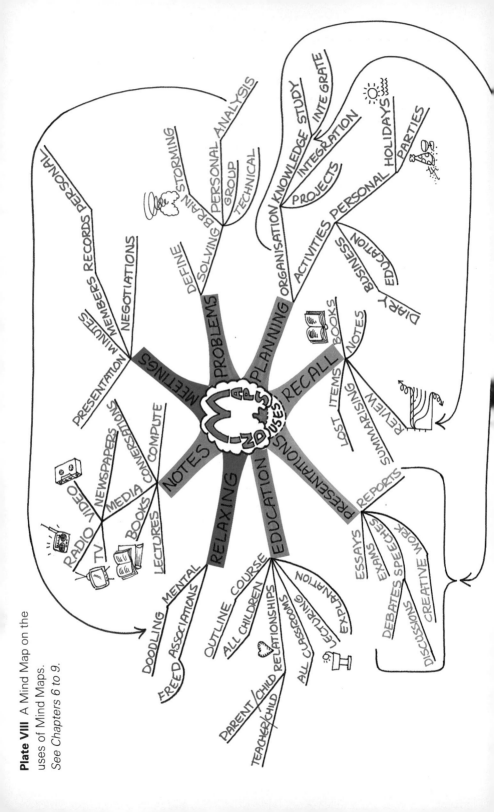

Plate VIII A Mind Map on the uses of Mind Maps. *See Chapters 6 to 9.*

Although this first attempt at mapping may have been a little unusual, you will probably have noticed that the experience is quite different from that of the first exercise, and that the problems too may have been quite different.

Problems often noted in the first exercise include;

order	**organisation**
logical sequence	**time distribution**
beginning	**emphasis of ideas**
ending	**mental blocking**

These problems arise because people are attempting to select the main headings and ideas one after the other, and are attempting to put them into order as they go – they are trying to order a structure of speech without having considered all the information available. This will inevitably lead to confusion and the problems noted, for new information which turns up after the first few items might suddenly alter the whole outlook on the subject. With a linear approach this type of happening is disruptive, but with the Mind Map approach it is simply part of the overall process, and can be handled properly.

Another disadvantage of the list-like method is that it operates against the way in which the brain works. Each time an idea is thought of it is put on the list and forgotten while a new idea is searched for. This means that all the multi-ordinate and associative possibilities of each word are cut off and boxed away while the mind wanders around in search of another new idea.

With the Mind Map approach each idea is left as a totally open possibility so that the map grows organically and increasingly, rather than being stifled.

You might find it interesting to compare your efforts so far with the efforts of three school children. *See figs 32 to 34 (pages 99–101).*

Figure 32, page 99 shows the normal writing of a fourteen-year-old boy who was described as reasonably bright, but messy, confused, and mentally disorganised. The example of his linear writing represents his 'best notes' and explains clearly why he was described as he was. The Mind Map of English which he completed in five minutes shows almost completely the reverse, suggesting that we can often misjudge a child by the method by which we require him to express himself.

Figure 33, page 100 is the Mind Map of a boy who twice failed 'O' level Economics and who was described by the teacher as having enormous thinking and learning problems combined with an almost total lack of knowledge of his subject. The Mind Map which also was completed in five minutes, shows quite the reverse.

Figure 34, page 101 is a Mind Map done by an 'A' Level grammar school girl on pure Mathematics. When this map was shown to a Professor of Mathematics he estimated that it was done by a University Honours student and that it probably took two days to complete. In fact it took the girl only 20 minutes. The Mind Map enabled her to display an extraordinary creativity in a subject which is normally considered dry, dull and oppressive. It could have been even better if each line had contained only 'units' of words instead of phrases. Her use of form and shape to augment the words will give an indication of the diversity possible in these structures. The following chapter extends this idea.

The Mind Map on Colour Plate III was done by a 13-year-old girl in California who, like Edward Hughes, was considered to be a 'normal' or 'average' student. The Mind Map, magnificently summarising both the content and also the feelings and emotions of the *Kusa-Hibari* story on pages 78–80, is a superb example of the way in which colour, code, form and image can be used to encapsulate an entire story.

The Mind Maps on Colour Plates IV–VII represent a new method for noting. They summarise chapters 2, 4, 5 and the chapters on Mind Mapping (6, 7, 8).

Page 102 has been left blank for you to create a Mind Map of chapter 7 for yourself.

In these Mind Maps, Key Recall Words and images are linked to each other around a main central image (in these cases, the overall theme of a chapter), and a mental picture is built up of an entire thought structure.

▶ The theory and method for making these Mind Maps are fully outlined in this chapter, starting on page 93.

▶ Use the Mind Map for each chapter as a **preview** of what is to come; they will make the reading of the chapter easier.

▶ After finishing a chapter, look at the Mind Map once again. This will serve as a **review,** and will help you to remember what you have read. Continue to review in accordance with the Review Timetable if you wish the information to be committed to your Long Term Memory.

7) SETTING   Time + places in which
the novel is situated

8) IMAGERY   the kind of images the
author uses to describe (usually by
simile or metaphor)

9) SYMBOLISM   one thing stands for
another
The witches in Macbeth signifying evil

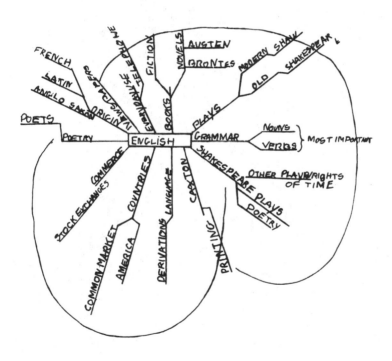

Fig 32 The 'best notes' in linear writing of a 14-year-old boy, and his Mind Map
notes on English. *See text page 97.*

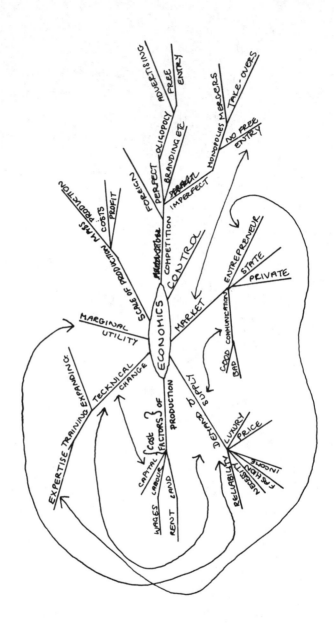

Fig 33 Mind Map by a boy who twice failed 'O' level Economics. *See text page 97.*

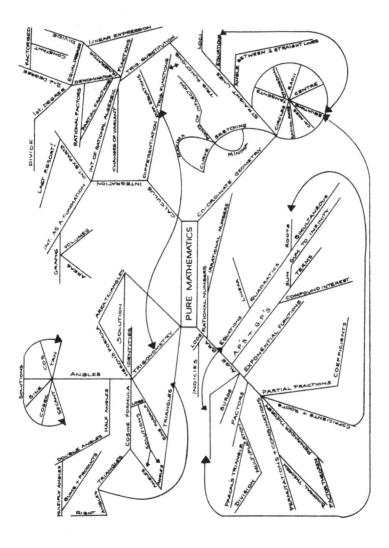

Fig 34 Mind Map by an 'A' level grammar school girl on pure Mathematics. *See text page 98.*

MAKE YOUR OWN MIND MAP OF CHAPTER SEVEN

Personal notes, Mind Maps and applications

8 Mind Maps – advanced methods and uses

OVERVIEW

► **Advanced Mind Maps**

► **Mind Maps and the left and right cortex**

► **Mind Maps – uses**

► **Mind Mapping for speeches and articles**

► **Mind Mapping for lectures**

► **Mind Mapping for meetings**

ADVANCED MIND MAPS

Combining the information from all previous chapters, and observing that the brain handles information better if the information is designed to 'slot in', and observing also the information from this chapter about the dimensional nature of the mind, it follows that notes which are themselves more 'holographic' and creative will be far more readily understood, appreciated and recalled.

There are many devices we can use to make such notes:

arrows
These can be used to show how concepts which appear on different parts of a pattern are connected. The arrow can be single or multi-headed and can show backward and forward directions.

codes
Asterisks, exclamation marks, crosses and question marks as well as many other indicators can be used next to words to show connections or other 'dimensions'.

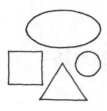

geometrical shapes
Squares, oblongs, circles, ellipses, etc. . . . can be used to mark areas or words which are similar in nature – for example triangles might be used to show areas of possible solution in a problem-solving pattern. Geometrical shapes can also be used to show order of importance. Some people, for example, prefer to use a square always for their main centre, oblongs for the ideas near the centre, triangles for ideas of next importance, and so on.

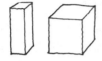

artistic three dimension
Each of the geometrical shapes mentioned, and many others, can be given perspective. For example, making a square into a cube. The ideas printed in these shapes will thus 'stand off' the page.

creativity images
Creativity can be combined with the use of dimension by making aspects of the pattern fit the topic. One man, for example, when doing a pattern on atomic physics, used the nucleus of an atom and the electrons that surrounded it, as the centre for his pattern.

colour
Colour is particularly useful as a memory and creative aid. It can be used, like arrows, to show how concepts which appear on different parts of the pattern are connected. It can also be used to mark off the boundaries between major areas of a pattern.

MIND MAPS AND THE LEFT AND RIGHT CORTEX

At this point it is useful to consider how recent research into the brain adds strength to the points raised so far. In light of the fact, as already outlined, that the brain handles information better if the information is designed to 'slot in', consider the left and right cortex research of Roger Sperry, Robert Ornstein and Eran Zaidel.

This research alone would lead you to conclude that a note-taking and thought-organisation technique designed to satisfy the needs of the whole brain would have to include not only words, numbers, sequence, and linearity, but also colour, dimension, visual rhythms, spatial awareness, etc: in other words Mind Maps.

From whatever perspective one approaches the question, be it from the nature of words and information, the function of recall, holographic models of the brain, or recent brain research, the conclusions in the end are identical – in order to fully utilise the brain's capacity, we need to consider each of the elements that add up to the whole, and integrate them in a unified way.

MIND MAPS – USES

The nature of Mind Maps is intimately connected with the function of the mind, and they can be used in nearly every activity where thought, recall, planning or creativity are involved. Colour Plate VIII is a Mind Map on the uses of Mind Maps, showing this wide variety of uses. In the remainder of this chapter I shall explain the application of Maps to the speech writing, essay writing, examination type of task; to meetings and communications, and to note taking.

MIND MAPPING FOR SPEECHES AND ARTICLES

Many people, when first shown Mind Maps, question if they can be used for any linear purpose, such as giving a talk or writing an article. If you refer to the Mind Map of this chapter on Plate VII, you will find how such a transformation took place:

Once the Mind Map has been completed, the required information is readily available. All that is necessary is to decide the final order in which to present the information. A good Mind Map will offer a number of possibilities. When the choice is being made, each area of the Mind Map can be encircled with a different colour, and numbered in the correct order. Putting this into written or verbal form is simply a matter of outlining the major areas to be covered, and then going through them point by point, following the logic of the branched connections. In this way the problem of redrafting and redrafting yet again is eliminated – all the gathering and organising will have been completed at the Mind Map stage.

It was using these techniques at Cambridge University that enabled Edward Hughes to complete his extraordinarily successful saga. It also enabled me to write *Use Your Head*!

MIND MAPPING FOR LECTURES

It is advisable, when taking notes, to use a large (A3) blank page, to enable your brain to see 'the whole picture' of the information which your mind is investigating.

When taking notes, especially from lectures, it is important to remember that Key words and images are essentially all that is needed. It is also important to remember that the final structure will not become apparent till the end. Any notes made will therefore probably be semi-final rather than final copy. The first few words noted may be fairly disconnected until the theme of the lecture becomes apparent. It is necessary to understand clearly the value of so-called 'messy' as opposed to 'neat' notes, for many people feel apprehension at having a scrawly, arrowed, non-linear page of notes developing in front of them. 'Neat' notes are traditionally those which are organised in an orderly and linear manner. *See fig 31* in the previous chapter. 'Messy' notes are those which are 'untidy' and 'all over the page'. The word 'messy' used in this way refers to the *look* and not to the *content*.

In note taking it is primarily the content and not the look that is of importance. The notes which look 'neat' are, in information terms, messy. As explained on page 85, the key information is disguised, disconnected, and cluttered with many informationally irrelevant words. The notes which look 'messy' are informationally far neater. They show immediately the important concepts, the connections, and even in some cases the crossings-out and the objections.

Mind Mapped notes in their final form are usually neat in any case and it seldom takes more than ten minutes to finalise an hour's notes on a fresh sheet of paper. The final Mind Map reconstructing is a productive exercise, particularly if the learning period has been organised properly so as to fit in perfectly as the first review. *See pages 64–66.*

MIND MAPPING FOR MEETINGS

Meetings, notably those for planning or problem solving, often degenerate into situations where each person listens to the others only in order to make his own point as soon as the previous speaker has finished. In such meetings many excellent points are passed over or forgotten, and much time is wasted. A further aggravation is that points which are finally accepted are not necessarily the best, but those made by the most vociferous or important speakers.

These problems can be eliminated if the person who organises the meeting uses a Mind Map structure. On a board at the front of the room the central theme of the discussion, together with a couple of the sub themes, should be presented in basic Mind Map form. The members of the meeting will have pre-knowledge of what it is about, and will hopefully have come prepared. As each member finishes the point he is making, he can be asked to summarise it in Key form, and to indicate where on the overall Mind Map he thinks his point should be entered.

The following are the advantages of this approach:

1 The contribution of each person is registered and recorded properly.

2 No information is lost.

3 The importance given to ideas will pertain more to what was said than to who said it.

4 People will be speaking more to the point, thereby eliminating digressions and long wafflings.

5 After the meeting each individual will have a Mind Mapped record and will therefore not have lost most of what is said by the following morning.

One further advantage of Mind Maps, especially in note taking and communications, is that the individual is kept continually and actively involved in the complete structure of what is going on, rather than being concerned solely with 'getting down' the last point made. The more complete involvement will lead to a much greater critical and analytical facility, a much greater integration, a much greater ability to recall and a much greater overall understanding.

Mind Maps are an external 'photograph' of the complex inter-relationships of your thought at any given time. They enable your brain to 'see itself' more clearly, and will greatly enhance the full range of your thinking skills: they will add increasing competence, enjoyment, elegance and fun to your life.

Personal notes and applications

The Mind Map Organic Study Technique (MMOST)

► **The reluctant learner**

► **The study book as a threat**

► **Old and new study techniques**

► **MMOST**

► **MMOST: Preparation**

► **MMOST: Application**

► **Summary: MMOST**

THE RELUCTANT LEARNER

The Six-o'clock-In-The-Evening-Enthusiastic-Determined-And-Well-Intentioned-Studier-Until-Midnight is a person with whom you are probably already familiar. At 6 o'clock he approaches his desk, and carefully organises everything in preparation for the study period to follow. Having everything in place he next carefully adjusts each item again, giving him time to complete the first excuse; he recalls that in the morning he did not have quite enough time to read all items of interest in the newspaper. He also realises that if he is going to study it is best to have such small items completely out of the way before settling down to the task at hand.

He therefore leaves his desk, browses through the newspaper and notices as he browses that there are more articles of interest than he had originally thought.•He also notices, as he leafs through the pages, the entertainment section. At this point it will seem like a good idea to plan for the evening's first break – perhaps an interesting half-hour programme between 8 and 8.30 pm.

He finds the programme, and it inevitably starts at about 7 pm.

At this point, he thinks 'well, I've had a difficult day and it's not too long before the programme starts, and I need a rest anyway and the relaxation will really help me to get down to studying. . . .' He returns to his desk at 7.45 pm, because the beginning of the next programme was also a bit more interesting than he thought it would be.

At this stage, he still hovers over his desk tapping his book reassuringly as he remembers that phone call to a friend which, like the articles of interest in the newspaper, is best cleared out of the way before the serious studying begins.

The phone call, of course, is much more interesting and longer than originally planned, but eventually the intrepid studier finds himself back at his desk at about 8.30 pm.

At this point in the proceedings he actually sits down at the desk, opens the book with a display of physical determination and starts to read (usually page one) as he experiences the first pangs of hunger and thirst. This is disastrous because he realises that the longer he waits to satisfy the pangs, the worse they will get, and the more interrupted his study concentration will be.

The obvious and only solution is a light snack. This, in its preparation, grows like the associative structure of a Mind Map, as more and more tasty items are linked to the central core of hunger. The snack becomes a feast.

Having removed this final obstacle the desk is returned to with the certain knowledge that this time there is nothing that could possibly interfere with the dedication. The first couple of sentences on page one are looked at again . . . as the studier realises that his stomach is feeling decidedly heavy and a general drowsiness seems to have set in. Far better at this juncture to watch that other interesting half-hour programme at 10 o'clock, after which the digestion will be mostly completed and the rest will enable him to *really* get down to the task at hand.

At 12 o'clock we find him asleep in front of the TV.

Even at this point, when he has been woken up by whoever comes into the room, he will think that things have not gone too badly, for after all he had a good rest, a good meal, watched some interesting and relaxing programmes, fulfilled his social commitments to his friends, digested the day's information, and got everything completely out of the way so that tomorrow, at 6 o'clock. . . .

THE STUDY BOOK AS A THREAT

The above episode is amusing, but the implications of it are significant and serious.

On one level the story is encouraging because, by the very fact that it is a problem experienced by everybody it confirms what has long been suspected: that everyone is creative and inventive, and that the feelings that many have about being uncreative are not necessary. The creativity demonstrated in the example of the reluctant student is not applied very usefully. But the diversity and originality with which we all make up reasons for *not* doing things suggests that each person has a wealth of talent which could be applied in more positive directions!

Fig 35 At the present time information is being given more importance and emphasis than the individual. As a result he is being mentally swamped and almost literally 'weighed down' by it all. Both the information and publication explosions are still continuing at staggering rates, while the ability of the individual to handle and study it all remains neglected. If he is ever to cope with the situation he must learn not more 'hard facts' but new ways of handling and studying the information – new ways of using his natural abilities to learn, think, recall, create, and solve problems. *See also fig 37 and text pages 116–118.*

On another level the story is discouraging because it shows up the wide-spread and underlying fear that most of us experience when confronted with a study text.

This reluctance and fear arises from the examination-based school system in which the child is presented with books on the subjects he is 'taking' at school. He knows that text books are 'harder' than story books and novels; he also knows that they represent a lot of work; and he further knows that he will be tested on his knowledge of the information from the books.

The fact that the type of book is 'hard' is discouraging in itself. The fact that the book represents work is also discouraging, because the child instinctively knows that he is unable to read, note, and remember properly.

And the fact that he is going to be tested is often the most serious of the three difficulties. It is well known that this threat can completely disrupt the brain's ability to work in certain situations. The number of cases are enormous of people who literally cannot write anything in an exam situation despite the fact that they know their subject thoroughly – as are the number of cases of people who, even though they are able to write some form of answer, have gigantic mental blocks where whole areas of knowledge are completely forgotten during an exam period. And in even more extreme cases many people have been known to spend a whole two hour period writing frantically, assuming that they were answering the question, but in fact repeating over and over again either their own name or one word.

Faced with this kind of threat, which for many is truly terrifying, the child has one of two choices: he can either study and face one set of consequences, or not study and face a different set of consequences. If he studies and does badly, then he has proven himself 'incapable', 'unintelligent', 'stupid', a 'dunce' or whatever the appropriate negative expression is at the time. Of course this is not really the case, but he has no way of knowing that it is the system which is not testing him properly, and not his own ineptitude causing the 'failure'.

If he does *not* study, the situation is quite different. Confronted with having failed a test or exam, he can immediately say that of course he failed it because he 'didn't study and wasn't interested in that kind of stuff anyway.'

By doing this, he solves the problem in a number of ways:

1 He avoids both the test and the threat to his self-esteem that studying would involve;

2 He has a perfect excuse for failing;

3 He gets respect from the other children because he is daring to attack a situation which is frightening to them. It is interesting to note that such a child will often find himself in the position of a leader.

It is also interesting to note that even those who do make the decision to study will still reserve a little part of themselves for behaving like the non-studier. The person who gets scores as high as 80 or 90 per cent will also be found using exactly the same excuses for not getting 100 per cent, as the non-studier uses for failing.

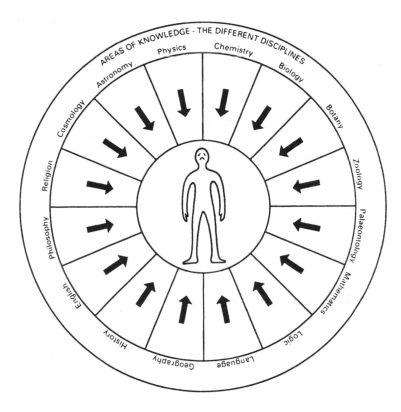

Fig 36 In traditional education information is given or 'taught' about the different areas of knowledge that surround the individual. The direction and flow is *from* the subject *to* the individual – he is simply given the information, and is expected to absorb, learn and remember as much as he possibly can. *See also fig 35 and text page 116.*

OLD AND NEW STUDY TECHNIQUES

The situations described above are unsatisfactory for everyone concerned, and have arisen for various reasons, many of them outlined in earlier parts of this book. One further and major reason for poor study results lies in the way we have approached both study techniques and the information we wanted people to study.

We have surrounded the person with a confusing mass of different subjects or 'disciplines' demanding that he learn, remember and understand a frightening array under headings such as Mathematics, Physics, Chemistry, Biology, Zoology, Botany, Anatomy, Physiology, Sociology, Psychology, Anthropology, Philosophy, History, Geography, Trigonometry, Palaeontology, etc. In each of these subject areas the individual has been and is still presented with series of dates, theories, facts, names, and general ideas. *See fig 36 (page 115).* What this really means is that we have been taking a totally lopsided approach to study and to the way in which a person deals with and relates to the information and knowledge that surrounds him. *See figs 36 (page 115) and 37 (opposite).*

As can be seen from the figures, we are concentrating far too much on information about the 'separate' areas of knowledge. We are also laying too much stress on asking the individual to feed back facts in pre-digested order or in pre-set forms such as standard examination papers or formal essays.

This approach has also been reflected in the standard study techniques recommended in Schools, Universities, Institutes of Further Education and text books. These techniques have been 'grid' approaches in which it is recommended that a series of steps always be worked through on any book being studied. One common suggestion is that any reasonably difficult study book should always be read through three times in order to ensure a complete understanding. This is obviously a very simple example, but even the many more developed approaches tend to be comparatively rigid and inflexible – simply standard systems to be repeated on each studying occasion.

It is obvious that methods such as these cannot be applied with success to every study book. There is an enormous difference between studying a text on Literary Criticism and studying a text on Higher Mathematics. In order to study properly, a technique is needed which does not force the same approach to such different materials.

First, it is necessary to start working from the individual outwards. Rather than bombarding him with books, formulas and examinations we must begin to concentrate on teaching each person how he or she *can* study most efficiently. We must teach ourselves how our eyes work when we read, how we remember, how we think, how we can learn more effectively, how we can organise noting, how we can solve problems and in general how we can best use our abilities, whatever the subject matter.

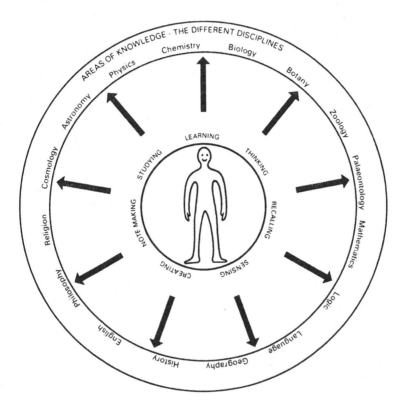

Fig 37 In the new forms of education, the previous emphases must be reversed. Instead of first teaching the individual facts about other things, we must first teach him facts about himself – facts about how he *can* learn, think, recall, create, solve problems etc. *See text opposite*.

One is tempted to note here that in our society we have Instruction Manuals and 'How To Do It' booklets on nearly everything, including the simplest of machines. But when it comes to the most complicated, complex, and important organism of all, ourselves, there has been practically no help. We need our own Owner's Manual on how to operate our own Super Bio Computer. Use Your Head is designed to be just that.

Most of the problems outlined in the first chapter will be eliminated when we finally do change the emphasis away from the subject toward the individual and how he can select and understand any information he wants to. People will be equipped to study and remember whatever area of knowledge is interesting or necessary. Things will not have to be 'taught to' or 'crammed in'. Each person will be able to range subjects at his own pace, going for help and personal supervision only when he realises it is necessary. *See fig 37 (page 117).*

Yet another advantage of this approach is that it will make both teaching and learning much easier, more enjoyable and more productive. By concentrating on the individual and his abilities we will finally and sensibly have placed the learning situation in its proper perspective.

MMOST

The Mind Map Organic Study Technique (MMOST) is divided into two main sections: Preparation and Application. Each of these sections is divided into four sub-sections:

Preparation   Browse
Time and Amount
Knowledge Mind Map
Questions and Goals

Application   Overview
Preview
Inview
Review

It is important to note at the outset that although the main steps are presented in a certain order, this order is by no means essential and can be changed, subtracted from and added to as the study texts warrant.

MMOST: PREPARATION

This first section contains:

- **The browse**
- **Time and amount**
- **Mind Map of knowledge on the subject**
- **Asking questions and defining goals**

The browse

Before doing anything else, it is *essential* to 'browse' or look through the entire book or periodical you are about to study. The browse should be done in the way you would look through a book you were considering buying in a bookshop, or in the way you would look through a book you were considering taking out from the library. In other words casually, but rather rapidly, flipping through the pages, getting the general 'feel' of the book, observing the organisation and structure, the level of difficulty, the proportion of diagrams and illustrations to text, the location of any results, summaries and conclusions sections etc.

Time and amount

These two aspects can be dealt with simultaneously because the theory behind them both is similar.

The first thing to do when sitting down to study a text book is to decide on the period of time to be devoted to it. Having done this decide what amount to cover in the time allocated.

The reason for insisting on these two initial steps is not arbitrary, and is supported by the findings of the *Gestalt* Psychologists. (Before reading on, complete the activity on page 120, figure 38.)

The *Gestalt* Psychologists discovered that the human brain has a very strong tendency to complete things – thus most readers will find that they labelled the shapes in figure 38 straight line, cylinder, square, ellipse or oval, zig-zag line, circle, triangle, wavy or curved line, rectangle. In fact the 'circle' is not a circle but a 'broken circle'. Many actually see this broken circle as a circle. Others see it as a broken circle but assume that the artist intended to complete it.

A more abstract example of our general desire to complete things is our universal tendency as children to build up a language that

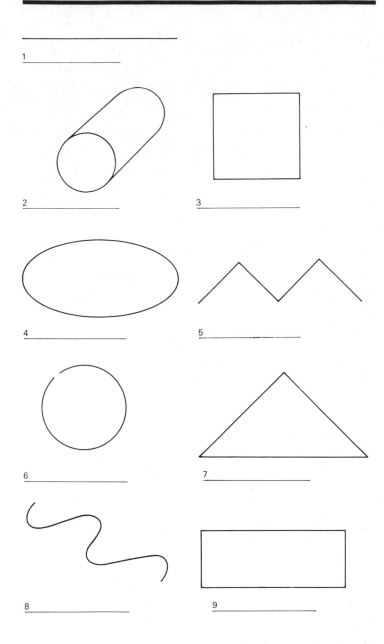

1 _____

2 _____   3 _____

4 _____   5 _____

6 _____   7 _____

8 _____   9 _____

Fig 38 Shape recognition.
Enter the name of the shape of each of the items above next to the appropriate number. *See text on page 119 after completion.*

helps us to make sense of, and form completed ideas of, our surroundings.

In study, making a decision about Time and Amount gives us immediate chronological and volume terrain, as well as an end point or goal. This has the added advantage of enabling the proper linkages to be made rather than encouraging a wandering off in more disconnected ways.

An excellent comparison is that of listening to a lecturer. A good lecturer who is attempting to expound a lot of difficult material will usually explain his starting and his ending points and will often indicate the amount of time he intends to spend on each area of his presentation. The audience will automatically find his lecture easier to follow because they have guide-lines within which to work.

It is advisable to define physically the amount to be read by placing reasonably large paper markers at the beginnings and end of the section chosen. This enables the reader to refer back and forward to the information in the amount chosen.

A further advantage of making these decisions at the outset is that the underlying fear of the unknown is avoided. If a large study book is plunged into with no planning, the reader will be continually oppressed by the number of pages he eventually has to complete. Each time he sits down he will be aware that he still has 'a few hundred pages to go' and will be studying with this as a constant and real background threat. If, on the other hand, he has selected a reasonable number of pages for the time he is going to study, he will be reading with the knowledge that the task he has set himself is easy and can certainly be completed. The difference in attitude and performance will be marked.

There are still further reasons for making these time and amount decisions which are concerned with the distribution of the reader's effort as time goes on.

Imagine that you have decided to study for two hours and that the first half-an-hour has been pretty difficult, although you have been making some progress. At this point in time you find that understanding begins to improve and that your progress seems to be getting better and faster.

Would you pat yourself on the back and take a break?

Or would you decide to keep the new and better rhythm going by studying on for a while until you began to lose the new impetus?

Ninety per cent of people asked those questions would carry on. Of those who would take a break, only a few would recommend the same thing to anyone else!

And yet surprisingly the best answer *is* to take a break. The reason for this can be seen by referring back to the discussion in the chapter on Memory and the amount that is recalled from a period of learning.

Despite the fact that understanding may be continually high, the recall of that understanding will be getting worse if the mind is not given a break, thus the graph, fig 20, is particularly relevant in the study situation. It is essential that any time period for studying be broken down into 20–50 minute sections with small rests in between. *See fig 21 (page 61).* The common student practice of swotting five hours at a stretch for examination purposes should become a thing of the past, for understanding is *not* the same as remembering, as all too many failed examination papers give witness.

The breaks themselves are also important for a number of reasons:

1 They give the body a physical rest and a chance to relax. This is always useful in a learning situation, and releases the build-up of tension.

2 They enable recall and understanding to 'work together' to the best advantage.

3 They allow a brief period of time for the just-studied information completely to relate each part of itself to the other part – to intra-integrate. *See fig 23 (page 63).*

This last point also relates to the Memory chapter and the graph on forgetting as time progresses. During each break the amount of knowledge that can immediately be recalled from the section just studied will increase and will be at a peak as the next section is commenced. This means that not only will more be recalled because the time period itself is best, but also that even more will be recalled because of the rest period.

To assist this even further, do a quick review of what you have read and a preview of what you are about to read at the beginning and end of each study period.

It has taken a number of pages to explain the necessity of deciding on a period of time and on an amount to be covered, but remember that the decisions themselves are extremely brief and will usually become automatic as you near completion of your browse. When these decisions have been made the next step can be taken:

● **Mind Map of knowledge on the subject**

Having decided on the amounts to be covered, next jot down as much as you know on the subject as fast as you can. No more than two minutes should be devoted to the exercise. Notes should be in Key words and in Mind Map form.

The purpose of this exercise is to improve concentration, to eliminate wandering, and to establish a good mental 'set'. This last term refers to getting the mind filled with important rather than unimportant information. If you have spent two minutes searching your memory for pertinent information, you will be far more attuned to the text material and far less likely to continue thinking about the strawberries and cream you are going to eat afterwards.

From the time limit of five minutes on this exercise it is obvious that a person's entire knowledge is not required on the pattern – the two minute exercise is intended purely to activate the storage system and to set the mind off in the right direction.

One question which will arise is 'what about the difference if I know almost nothing on the subject or if I know an enormous amount?' If knowledge in the area is great, the five minutes should be spent forming a pattern of the major divisions, theories, names etc. connected with the subject. As the mind can flash through information much faster than the hand can write it, all the minor associations will still be mentally 'seen' and the proper mental set and direction will be established.

If the knowledge of the subject is almost nothing, the two minutes should be spent patterning those few items which are known, as well as any other information which seems in any way at all to be connected. This will enable the reader to get as close as he possibly can to the new subject, and will prevent him from feeling totally lost as so many do in this situation.

Apart from being immediately useful in study, a continued practice with patterning information gives a number of more general advantages. First, the individual gains by gathering together his immediate and current state of knowledge on areas of interest. In this way he will be able to keep much more up to date with himself and will actually know what he knows, rather than being in a continually embarrassing position of not knowing what he knows – the 'I've got it on the tip of my tongue' syndrome.

In addition, this continued practice of recalling and integrating ideas gives enormous advantage in situations where such abilities are essential: examinations, impromptu speeches and answering on the spot questions, to name but a few.

Once the five-minute period is up, the next stage should be moved to immediately.

● Asking questions and defining goals

Having established the current state of knowledge on the subject, it is next advisable to decide what you want from the book. This involves defining the questions you want answered during the reading. The questions should be asked in the context of goals aimed for and should, like noting of knowledge, be done in Key Word and Mind Map form. Many prefer to use a different coloured pen for this section, and rather than starting a new map they add their questions to the already existing map on current knowledge.

This exercise, again like that for noting knowledge, is based on the principle of establishing proper mental sets. It should also take not much more than five minutes at the outset, as questions can be redefined and added to as the reading progresses.

A standard experiment to confirm this approach takes two groups of people who are generally equal in terms of age, education, aptitude etc. Each group is given the same study text and is given enough time to complete the whole book.

Group A is told that they are going to be given a completely comprehensive test on everything in the book and that they must study accordingly.

Group B is told that they will be tested on two or three major themes which run through the book, and that they also must study accordingly.

Both groups are in fact tested on the entire text, a situation which one would immediately think unfair to the group that had been told they would be tested only on the main themes.

One might also think that in this situation the second group would do better on questions about the themes they had been given, the first group better on other questions and that both groups might have a similar final score.

To the surprise of many, the second group not only does better on questions about the themes, but they achieve higher total scores which include better marks on all parts of the test.

The reason for this is that the main themes act like great grappling hooks through the information, attaching everything else to them. In other words the main questions and goals acted as associative and linking centres to which all other information became easily attached.

The group instructed to get everything had no centres at all to connect new information to, and because of this was groping with no foundations through the information. It is much like a situation where a person is given so much choice that he ends up making no decision; the paradox where attempting to get everything gains nothing.

Asking questions and establishing goals can be seen, like the section preceding it, to become more and more important as the theory behind becomes better understood. It should be emphasised that the more accurately these questions and goals are established, the more able the reader will be to perform well in the Application section of the Mind Map Organic Study Technique.

MMOST: APPLICATION

This second section deals with **application** and contains:

- **Overview**
- **Preview**
- **Inview**
- **Review**
- **Text notes and Mind Mapping**
- **Continuing review**

● **Overview**

One of the interesting facts about people using study books is that most, when given a new text, start reading on page one. It is *not* advisable to start reading a new study text on the first page. The following situation is a parallel illustration of this point:

Imagine that you are a fanatical jigsaw-puzzle-doer. A friend arrives on your doorstep with a gigantic box wrapped in paper and tied with string, and tells you that it's a present: 'the most beautiful and complex jigsaw puzzle yet devised by man!'. You thank her, and as you watch her walk away down the front path, you decide that from that moment on you are going to devote yourself *entirely* to the completion of the puzzle.

Before continuing, note in *precise detail* the steps you would take from that point on in order to complete the task.

Now check your own answers with the following list compiled from my students:

1 Go back inside the house.
2 Take the string off the box.
3 Take off the paper.
4 Dispose of string and paper.
5 Look at the picture on the outside of the box.
6 Read the instructions, concentrating on number of pieces and overall dimensions of the puzzle.
7 Estimate and organise amount of time necessary for completion.
8 Plan breaks and meals!
9 Find surface of appropriate dimensions for puzzle.
10 Open box.
11 Empty contents of box onto surface or separate tray.
12 If pessimistic, check number of pieces!
13 Turn all pieces right side up.
14 Find edge and corner pieces.
15 Sort out colour areas.
16 Fit 'obvious' bits and pieces together.
17 Continue to fill in.
18 Leave 'difficult' pieces to end (for reason that as the overall picture becomes more clear, and the number of pieces used increases, so does the probability increase that the difficult pieces will fit in much more easily when there is greater context into which they *can* fit).
19 Continue process until completion.
20 Celebrate!

This jigsaw analogy can be applied directly to study, in the first instance making it clearer why it is so important not to commence studying on page one, as doing so would be like finding the bottom left-hand corner, and insisting to yourself that the entire picture be built up step by step from the corner only.

What is essential in a reasonable approach to study texts, especially difficult ones, is to get a good idea of what's in them before plodding on into a learning catastrophe. The overview is designed to perform this task, and may be likened to looking at the picture, reading the instructions, and finding the edge and corner pieces of the puzzle. What this means in the study context is that you should scour the book for all material not included in the regular body of the print, using your visual guide as you do so. Areas of the book to be covered in your overview include:

results	tables	subheadings
summaries	table of contents	dates
conclusions	marginal notes	italics
indents	illustrations	graphs
glossaries	capitalised words	footnotes
back cover	photographs	statistics

The function of this is to provide you with a good knowledge of the graphic sections of the book, not skimming the whole thing, but selecting specific areas for relatively comprehensive coverage. *See fig 39.* At this time complete the central image and main branches of your Mind Map.

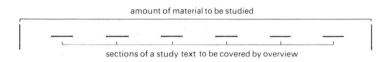

amount of material to be studied

sections of a study text to be covered by overview

Fig 39 Sections of a study text to be covered by overview. *See text above.*

It is extremely important to note again that throughout the overview a pen, pencil, or other form of visual guide should always be used.

The reason for this can best be explained by reference to a graph. If the eye is unaided, it will simply fixate briefly on general areas of the graph, then move off, leaving only a vague visual memory and an interference to that memory because the eye movement will not have 'registered' the same pattern as the graph.

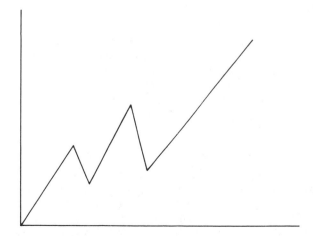

Fig 40 Example pattern of graph to be studied.

If a visual aid is used, the eye will more nearly approximate the flow of the graph and the memory will be strengthened by each of the following inputs:

1 The visual memory itself.
2 The remembered eye movement approximating the graph shape.
3 The memory of the movement of the arm or hand in tracing the graph (Kinaesthetic memory).
4 The visual memory of the rhythm and movement of the tracer.

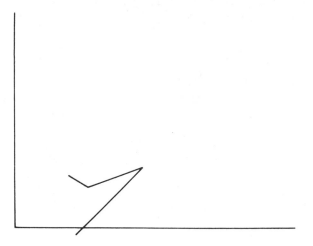

Fig 41 Standard pattern of unguided eye movement on graph causing conflicting memory of shape of graph.

The overall recall resulting from this practice is far superior to that of a person who reads without any visual guide. It is interesting to note that accountants often use their pens to guide their eyes across and down columns and rows of figures. They do this naturally because any very rigid linear eye movement is difficult to maintain with the unaided eye.

● Preview

The second section of study application is the preview – covering all that material not covered in the overview. In other words the paragraphed, language content of the book. This can be likened to organising the colour areas of your puzzle.

During the preview, concentration should be directed to the beginnings and ends of paragraphs, sections, chapters, and even whole texts, because information tends to be concentrated at the beginnings and ends of written material.

If you are studying a short academic paper or a complex study book, the Summary Results and Conclusion sections should always be read first. These sections often include exactly those essences of information that you are searching for, enabling you to grasp that essence without having to wade through a lot of time-wasting material.

Having gained the essence from these sections, simply check that they do indeed summarise the main body of the text.

In the preview, as with the overview, you are not fully reading all the material, but simply concentrating once again on special areas. *See fig 42 (below)*.

amount of material to be studied

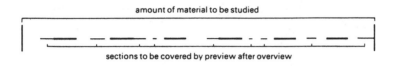

sections to be covered by preview after overview

Fig 42 Sections to be covered by preview after overview. *Again add any appropriate information or references to your Mind Map. See text this page.*

The value of this section cannot be overemphasised. A case in point is that of a student taught at Oxford who had spent four months struggling through a 500-page tome on psychology. By the time he had reached page 450 he was beginning to despair because the amount of information he was 'holding on to' as he tried to get to the end was becoming too much – he was literally beginning to drown in the information just before reaching his goal.

It transpired that he had been reading straight through the book, and even though he was nearing the end, did not know what the last chapter was about. It was a complete summary of the book! He read the section and estimated that had he done so at the beginning he would have saved himself approximately 70 hours in reading time, 20 hours in note-taking time and a few hundred hours of worrying.

In both the overview and preview you should very actively **select** and reject. Many people still feel obliged to read everything in a book even though they know it is not necessarily relevant to them. It is far better to treat a book in the way most people treat lecturers. In other words, if the lecturer is boring skip what he says, and if he is giving too many examples, is missing the point or is making errors, select, criticise, correct, and disregard as appropriate.

● Inview

After the overview and preview, and providing that still more information is required, inview the material. This involves 'filling in' those areas still left, and can be compared with the filling in process of the jigsaw puzzle, once the boundaries and colour areas have been established. It is *not* necessarily the major reading, as in some cases most of the important material will have been covered in the previous stages.

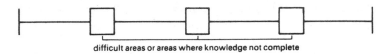

difficult areas or areas where knowledge not complete

Fig 43 Sections covered after inview has been completed. As you proceed, add the relevant information to your Mind Map. *See text this page.*

It should be noted from fig 43 (*above*) that there are still certain sections which have been left incomplete even at the inview stage. This is because it is far better to move *over* particularly difficult points than to batter away at them immediately from one side only.

Once again the comparison with the jigsaw puzzle becomes clear: racking your brains to find the pieces that connect to your 'difficult bit' is a tension-producing waste of time, and jamming the piece in, or cutting it with a pair of scissors so that it *does* fit (assuming or pretending you understand in context when *really* you don't) is similarly futile. The difficult sections of a study text are seldom essential to that which follows them, and the advantages of leaving them are manifold:

1 If they are not immediately struggled with, the brain is given that most important brief period in which it can work on them sub-consciously. (Most readers will have experienced the examination question which they 'can't possibly answer' only to find on returning to the question later that the answer pops out and often seems ridiculously simple.)

2 If the difficult areas are returned to later, they can be approached from both sides. Apart from its obvious advantages, considering the difficult area in context (as with the difficult bit in the jigsaw) also enables the brain's automatic tendency to fill in gaps to work to greater advantage.

3 Moving on from a difficult area releases the tension and mental floundering that often accompanies the traditional approach.

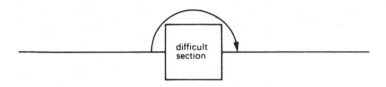

Fig 44 'Jumping over' a stumbling block usually enables the reader to go back to it later on with more information from 'the other side'. The block itself is seldom essential for the understanding of that which follows it. *See text opposite.*

An adjunct to this last point is that it tends to make studying a more creative process.

Looking at the normal historical development of any discipline, it is found that a fairly regular series of small and logically connected steps are interrupted by great leaps forward.

The propounders of these giant new steps have in many cases 'intuited' them (combining left and right cortex functions, as outlined in chapter 2), and afterwards been met with scorn. Galileo and Einstein are examples. As they then explained their ideas step by step, others gradually and progressively understood, some early in the explanation, and others as the innovator neared his conclusion.

In the same manner in which the innovator jumps over an enormous number of sequential steps, and in the same manner in which those who first realised his conclusions did so, the studier who leaves out small sections of study will be giving a greater range to his natural creative and understanding abilities. *See fig 45* (*below*).

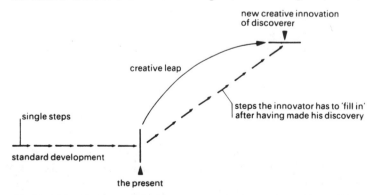

Fig 45 Historical development of ideas and creative innovations. *See text this page.*

● Review

Having completed the overview, preview and inview, and if further information is still required to complete goals, answer questions or solve problem areas, a review stage is necessary.

In this stage simply fill in all those areas as yet incomplete, and reconsider those sections marked as noteworthy. In most cases it will be found that not much more than 70 per cent of that initially considered relevant will finally be used. Then complete your Mind Map notes.

● Text notes and Mind Mapping

Noting while studying takes two main forms:
1 Notes made on the text itself.
2 A growing Mind Map.

1 Notes you make in the book itself can include:

1 Underlining.
2 Personal thoughts generated by the text.
3 Critical comments.
4 Marginal straight lines for important or note-worthy material.
5 Curved or wavy marginal lines to indicate unclear or difficult material.
6 Question marks for areas that you wish to question or that you find questionable.
7 Exclamation marks for outstanding items.
8 Your own symbol code for items and areas that relate to your own specific and general objectives.
9 Mini Mind Maps in the margins.

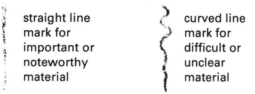

straight line mark for important or noteworthy material

curved line mark for difficult or unclear material

Fig 46 Techniques for marking text.

If the book is not valuable, markings can be made in colour codes. If the book is a cherished volume, then markings can be made with a very soft pencil. If the pencil is soft enough, and if a *very* soft eraser is used, the damage to the book will be less than that caused by the finger and thumb as they turn a page.

2 The growing Mind Map

You will find that Mind Mapping the structure of the text as you progress through it is very similar to building up the picture of the jigsaw puzzle as you fit in bit by bit. Ideally the bulk of Mind Map noting should take place during the latter stages of study, as in the earlier stages it is very difficult to know what is *definitely* note-worthy, and subsequently unnecessary noting can be avoided.

It is best to start with a central image that captures the essence of that which you are studying, and from that central image, to branch out with the major sub-subject headings or chapter headings forming the central arms from which the secondary and tertiary levels of your note taking will emanate. *Re-read now chapter 7, 'Mind Mapping laws', starting on page 95.*

The advantage of building up a Mind Map as you progress through the study text is that you externalise and integrate a lot of information that would otherwise be 'up-in-the-air'. The growing Mind Map also allows you to refer back quickly to areas you have previously covered, rather than having to thumb through pages already read.

It will enable you after a reasonable amount of basic study, to see just where the areas of confusion in your subject are, and to see also where your subject connects with other subjects. As such it will place you in the creative situation of being able to: integrate the known; realise the relevance to other areas; and to make appropriate comment where confusion and debate still exist. The final stage of your study will include the completion and integration of any notes from your text with the Mind Map, which will act as your basis for ongoing study and review.

When you have completed this final stage, you should, as did our imaginary jigsaw puzzle fanatic, celebrate! This may sound humorous, but it is also serious: if you associate the completion of study tasks with personal celebration, the context of your study will become increasingly more pleasant, and thus the probability of your studying far greater.

Once your study programme is well under way, it is advisable to keep enormous 'Master' Mind Maps which summarise and overview the main branches and structures of your subject areas.

● Continuing review

Apart from the immediate review, a continuing review programme is essential, and should be constructed in the light of the knowledge we have concerning memory as discussed in the chapter on Memory.

It was seen that memory did not decline immediately after a learning situation, but actually rose before levelling off and then plummeting.

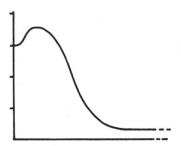

Fig 47 Graph showing that memory actually rises after learning, before declining sharply. *See text this page.*

This graph can be warped to your advantage by reviewing just at that point where the memory starts to fall. A review here, at the point of highest memory and integration, will keep the high point up for another one or two days and so on as explained on page 64. *See also fig 24 (page 65).*

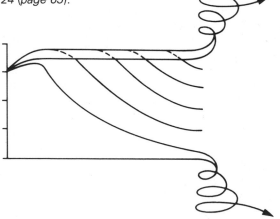

Fig 48 This graph shows how quickly forgetting takes place after something has been learned. It also shows how review can 'warp' this graph to enormous advantage. *See text this page.*

SUMMARY: THE MIND MAP ORGANIC STUDY TECHNIQUE

The entire Mind Map Organic Study Technique must be seen not as a step by step progression, but as a series of inter-related aspects of approaching study material. It is quite possible to switch and change the order from the one given here. The amount to be covered may be decided upon before the period of time; the subject matter may be known before the time and amount are decided upon and consequently the knowledge Mind Map could be completed first; the questions can be asked at the preparation stage or after any one of the latter stages; the overview can be eliminated in books where it is inappropriate, or repeated a number of times if the subjects were mathematics or physics. (One student found that it was easier to read four chapters of post-degree mathematics 25 times per week for four weeks quickly using the survey technique, than to struggle through one formula at a time. He was of course applying to its extreme, but very effectively, the point made about skipping over difficult areas.) Preview can be eliminated or broken down into separate sections; and the inview and review can be variously extended or eliminated.

In other words each subject, and each book of each subject, can be confidently approached in the manner best suited to it. To each book you will bring the knowledge that whatever the difficulties, you possess the fundamental understanding to choose the appropriate and necessarily unique approach.

Study is consequently made a personal, interactive, continually changing and stimulating experience, rather than a rigid, impersonal and tiresomely onerous task.

It should also be noted that despite the apparently greater number of 'times the book is being read' this is *not* the case. By using the Mind Map Organic Study Technique you will be on average reading most sections once only and will then be effectively reviewing those sections considered important. A pictorial representation can be seen in fig 49 (*below*).

Fig 49 'Number of times' book is covered using Mind Map Organic Study Technique. *See text this page.*

By contrast, the 'once through' reader is *not* reading it once through but is reading it an enormous number of times. He thinks he is reading it through once only because he takes in once piece of information after another. He does not realise that his regressions, back-skipping, re-reading of difficult sentences, general disorganisation and forgetting because of inadequate review, result in an actual reading of the book or chapter as many as ten times.

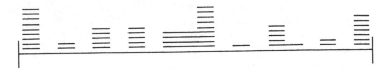

Fig 50 'Number of times' book is covered using traditional 'once through' reading techniques. *See text this page.*

The Mind Map Organic Study Technique will allow you easy and delightful access to the world of knowledge in a manner that will encourage your brain to learn more and more easily as it learns more, and will turn you from a reluctant learner to one who will, like Edward Hughes, avidly devour books by the hundred!

Personal notes, Mind Maps and application

10 Directions

WHAT A DIFFERENCE TWENTY-ONE YEARS CAN MAKE

As the twentieth century ends, the human race, with many members still not realising it, has entered what will probably be considered by future historians as the beginning of the greatest Renaissance ever, and one which will arguably become a permanent feature of human evolution.

In the fifteen years since I first wrote *Use Your Head*, there has been a worldwide explosion of interest in art, theatre, music, the sciences, general knowledge, the exploration of our terrestrial, extra-terrestrial and Universal environments, and, perhaps most of all, our fascination with and accelerating investigation of our own intelligence.

Old beliefs are disintegrating in the glare of our knowledge about ourselves. Take, for example, ideas about the way human mental ability declines with age.

REVIEW, MENTAL ABILITY AND AGE

The way in which a person reviews has an interesting connection with popular ideas about the way human mental ability declines with age. It is normally assumed that IQ scores, recall ability, ability to see special relationships, perceptual speed, speed of judgement, induction, figural relations, associative memory, intellectual level, intellectual speed, semantic relations, formal and general reasoning etc., decline after reaching a peak at the age of 18 to 25 (*see fig 51, below*). Valid as the figure produced may be, two important factors must be noted:

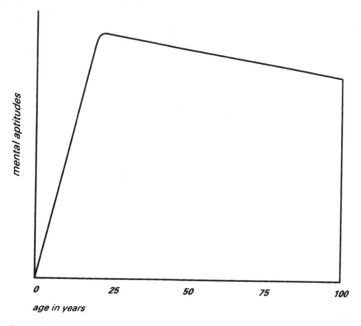

Fig 51 Graph showing standard results of measuring mental aptitudes as a person gets older. It is assumed that after reaching a peak at approximately 18–25, decline is thereafter slow but steady. *See text on previous page.*

1 The decline over the life-time is little more than 5 to 10 per cent. When considered in relation to the brain's enormous inherent capacity, this is insignificant.

2 The people who took part in the experiments which arrived at these discouraging figures had been educated traditionally, and therefore in most cases would not have been practising proper learning, reviewing and remembering techniques.

Looking at figure 51 it can be easily seen that such a person's mental 'conditioning' would have been at a very low level for an increasing number of years. In other words his real intellectual capacities would have been in 'cold storage'. It is not surprising that such an unused mind would do slightly worse after 20 to 40 years of mis- or no use – it is surprising that it still manages to do as well as it does!

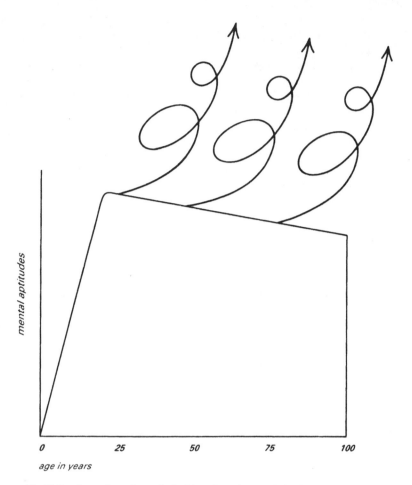

Fig 52 Graphs such as shown in fig 51 are based on statistics from people taught traditionally. A human being would naturally tend to improve these capacities with age if taught in a manner that complemented and nourished the brain's natural functioning.

If, on the other hand, the mind were continually used, and its capacities expanded, the effect on the graph for age would be dramatic. This can be seen by taking note of those older people who have remained active and explorative rather than assuming that they were going to get worse as the years passed. Very often their recall is almost total, and their ability to understand and learn new areas of knowledge far surpasses that of equally enthusiastic but younger and less experienced minds. *See fig 52 (above).*

In studying human mental performance it has been mistakenly assumed that the decline found with age is 'natural' and unavoidable. Instead a closer look should be taken at the people being studied, and then experiments should be performed to find out how abilities can be maximised rather than minimised.

Increasingly we are finding positive **'Renegades from the Norm':** people over the age of 70 whose defining characteristics are: vitality, optimism, humour, physical strength, persistence, mischievousness, enthusiasm, interest, expanding knowledge, curiosity, kindness, exhaustive memory and sensuality. The very characteristics that one would ascribe to children.

We are finding that if we understand, care for and 'use our heads' in the way they were designed, the Edward Hughes Story will become the Every Child Story.

Afterword

As you approach the end of *Use Your Head* I hope that you will be realising that it is not the end, but the real beginning. With the physical beauty and complexity of your brain, and its enormous intellectual and emotional powers, with your ability to absorb information and to manage the memorisation of that information, and with the new techniques for allowing your brain to express and organise itself in matters which are more comprehensibly attuned to the way you function, reading, studying, learning, and life in general should become what they can be: delightful and flowing processes that bring not pain and frustration, but pleasure and fulfilment.

Anyone interested in further reading or in courses dealing with the subject covered in *Use Your Head* can contact the author c/o:

Buzan Centres Limited,
37 Waterloo Road,
Bournemouth,
Dorset
BH9 1BD

Tel: 01202 533593
Fax: 01202 534572

Appendix

THE BRAIN CLUB

The Brain Club is an international organisation designed to help you increase your mental, physical and spiritual awareness. This is done by waking that sleeping giant, your Brain, and teaching you how to access its vast intelligences, first by Learning How to Learn and then by developing specific skills in areas that you choose.

You can do this by studying in your own home, or meeting regularly with others who also wish to expand their vast range of mental skills as outlined in *Use Your Head*.

Join these 'mental gymnasiums' and improve the following skills:

a Memorising
b Range/Speed Reading
c Mind Mapping and Creative Thinking
d Learning and Studying
e IQ
f Mathematics
g The Arts
h Physical performance
i Vocabulary Building/Language Learning
j Communicating
k Personality Development
l Games skills
m Specialist skills

Each area within The Brain Club will be graded and certificates awarded as you reach advancing levels of competence. For details of the nearest Cell of The Brain Club, contact:

The Buzan Centre
Suite 2, Cardigan House, 37 Waterloo Road, Winton,
Dorset BH9 1BD. Telephone: 0202 533593 Fax: 0202 534572

PRODUCTS

Audiotapes

Learning and Memory – produced for *Psychology Today* magazine.

The Intelligence Revolution (set of 3 tapes)
Tony Buzan on Memory and Advanced Mind Mapping.

Make the Most of Your Mind – based on the book of the same name, and *Use Your Head*.

Supercreativity and Mind Mapping – a comprehensive introduction to the workings of your brain, and the theory and use of Mind Mapping (with mini-manual).

Videotapes

Use Your Head – the original nine-part BBC TV series attractively presented with updated facilitator's manual and *Use Your Head* and *Use Your Memory* books.

The Enchanted Loom – documentary on the brain featuring interviews with the world's major contributors to the field, devised and presented by Tony Buzan.

Buzan Business Training – complete business training course emphasising the application of Mind Mapping, Memory and Information Management to business.

Family Genius Training – complete video series based on *Use Your Head* and *Make the Most of Your Mind*, which guides the family through the latest information on the brain and brain training.

Posters

'Body and Soul' Master Mind Map poster – a limited edition poster depicting, in a surrealist manner, all the principles taught by Tony Buzan. This beautiful picture is called 'Body and Soul' and each numbered copy is signed by the Swedish artist, Ulf Ekberg.

'Brain' Cartoons by Pecub.

Thinking Cap by Lorraine Gill.

Mind Map Kits

Specially designed A3 & A4 pads and pens.

Master Your Memory Matrix 0–10,000

Laminated 0–99 and 100 to 10,000 Matrix plus full instructions to assist the *Master Your Memory Reader*.

To order, contact:

The Buzan Centre
Suite 2, Cardigan House, 37 Waterloo Road, Winton,
Dorset BH9 1BD. Telephone: 0202 533593 Fax: 0202 534572

THE UNIVERSAL PERSONAL ORGANISER (UPO)

This *new* and *unique* approach to time and self management is a diary system, based on the techniques created and taught by Tony Buzan.

The Universal Personal Organiser is a living system that grows with you, and that provides a comprehensive perspective on your life, your desires, and your business and family functions.

The Universal Personal Organiser is the first diary system to use the principles that Leonardo da Vinci discovered in the Italian Renaissance: that images and colour enhance both *creativity* and *memory*, as well as being more *enjoyable* and *easier* than regular diary systems.

The Universal Personal Organiser *reflects you*, and gives you the *freedom* to perform at your Highest Potential. The Universal Personal Organiser is made of materials that are to the *highest quality*, using the best leathers and paper available.

The Universal Personal Organiser is designed to help you manage the four main areas of life: *health* (mental, physical and emotional); *happiness (family); creativity;* and *wealth*.

The Universal Personal Organiser, in so doing, allows you to *organise* your past, present and future in a manner that is both *enjoyable* and *fun*.

The Universal Personal Organiser's pages and partitions have been designed to enable you to get a comprehensive perspective on your *yearly plan*, your *monthly* and *weekly plans*, and your *daily plan*, using the new *24 hour diary clock, Mind Mapping*, and *Use Your Head* systems.

BUZAN TRAINING COURSES

Courses are prepared for:
- ▶ Governments
- ▶ Corporations
- ▶ Schools and universities
- ▶ Private groups and organisations
- ▶ Foundations
- ▶ Children
- ▶ Families
- ▶ Senior citizens

The courses are based on the following books by Tony Buzan:
- ▶ *Use Your Head*
- ▶ *Use Your Memory*
- ▶ *Make the Most of Your Mind*
- ▶ *Master Your Memory*
- ▶ *Speed (and Range) Reading*
- ▶ *The Brain User's Guide*
- ▶ *Harnessing the ParaBrain*
- ▶ *Universal Personal Organiser*

The courses emphasise:
- ▶ Mind Mapping
- ▶ Memory skills – advanced
- ▶ Speed reading – advanced
- ▶ Learning to learn
- ▶ Creativity
- ▶ Presentation skills
- ▶ Work/study skills
- ▶ Corporate and family brain training
- ▶ The ageing brain
- ▶ Managing change
- ▶ Personal and time management
- ▶ Especially tailored courses

For enquiries, contact:

The Buzan Centre
Suite 2, Cardigan House, 37 Waterloo Road, Winton,
Dorset BH9 1BD.
Telephone: 0202 533593 Fax: 0202 534572

FOR FURTHER INFORMATION ON:

▶ Training courses based on Tony Buzan's methods
▶ Co-ordination of The Brain Club
▶ Supportive books, tapes and educational products

contact:

The Buzan Centre
Suite 2, Cardigan House, 37 Waterloo Road, Winton,
Dorset BH9 1BD.
Telephone: 0202 533593 Fax: 0202 534572

Please send a stamped, self-addressed envelope for
your reply.

ACKNOWLEDGEMENTS

The illustration on page 16 is from *The Organisation of the Brain* by
Walle J. H. Nauta and Michael Feirtag, copyright © September 1979 by
SCIENTIFIC AMERICAN Inc. All rights reserved.

Black and white illustrations: A1 Creative Services; Lorraine Gill; Mike Gilkes;
Pep Reiff; Robert Walster
Colour plates: Bob Harvey (Plate I), Robert Walster (Plate II),
Pep Reiff (Plates IV–VIII)

Mind Map plates designed by Vanda North

Bibliography

Atkinson, Richard C., and Shiffrin, Richard M. 'The Control of Short-term Memory.' *Scientific American*, August 1971.

Baddeley, Alan D. *The Psychology of Memory*. New York: Harper & Row, 1976.

Borges, Jorge L. *Fictions* (especially *Funes, the Memorious*). London: J. Calder, 1985.

Brown, Mark. *Memory Matters*. Newton Abbot: David & Charles, 1977.

Brown, R., and McNeil, D. 'The "Tip-of-the-Tongue" Phenomenon.' *Journal of Verbal Learning and Verbal Behavior* **5,** 325–37.

Buzan, Tony. *The Brain User's Guide*. New York: E. P. Dutton, 1983.

Buzan, Tony. *Make the Most of Your Mind*. London: Pan, 1988.

Buzan, Tony. *Master Your Memory*. Newton Abbot: David & Charles, 1988.

Buzan, Tony. *Memory Visions*. Newton Abbot: David & Charles, 1989.

Buzan, Tony. *Use Your Memory*. London: BBC Books, 1989.

Buzan, Tony. *Speed (and Range) Reading*. Newton Abbott: David & Charles, 1988.

Ebbinghaus, H. *Über das Gedächtnis*. Leipzig: Duncker, 1885. op.

Gelb, Michael. *Present Yourself*. London: Aurum Press, 1988.

Haber, Ralph N. 'How We Remember What We See.' *Scientific American*, May 1970, 105.

Howe, J. A., and Godfrey, J. *Student Note-Taking as an Aid to Learning*. Exeter: Exeter University Teaching Services, 1977. op.

Howe, M. J. A. 'Using Students' Notes to Examine the Role of the Individual Learner in Acquiring Meaningful Subject Matter.' *Journal of Educational Research* **64,** 61–3.

Hunt, E., and Love, T. 'How Good Can Memory Be?' in *Coding Processes in Human Memory*, pp. 237–60, edited by A. W. Melton and E. Martin. Washington, DC: Winston/Wiley, 1972. op.

Hunter, I. M. L. 'An exceptional memory.' *British Journal of Psychology* **68,** 155–64, 1977.

Keves, Daniel. *The Minds of Billy Milligan.* New York: Random House, 1981; London: Bantam, 1982.

Loftus, E. F. *Eyewitness Testimony.* Cambridge, Mass.: Harvard University Press, 1980.

Luria, A. R. *The Mind of a Mnemonist.* Cambridge, Mass.: Harvard University Press, 1987.

Penfield, W., and Perot, P. 'The Brain's Record of Auditory and Visual Experience: A Final Summary and Discussion.' *Brain* **86,** 595–702.

Penfield, W., and Roberts, L. *Speech and Brain-Mechanisms.* Princeton, NJ: Princeton University Press, 1959. op.

Penry, J. *Looking at Faces and Remembering Them: A Guide to Facial Identification.* London: Elek Books, 1971. op.

Ruger, H. A., and Bussenius, C. E. *Memory.* New York: Teachers College Press, 1913. op.

Russell, Peter. *The Brain Book.* London: Routledge & Kegan Paul, 1966; Ark, 1984.

Standing, Lionel. 'Learning 10,000 Pictures.' *Quarterly Journal of Experimental Psychology* **25,** 207–22.

Stratton, George M. 'The Mnemonic Feat of the "Shass Pollak".' *Physiological Review* **24,** 244–7.

Suzuki, S. *Nurtured by love: a new approach to education.* New York: Exposition Press, 1969.

Thomas, E. J. 'The Variation of Memory with Time for Information Appearing During a Lecture.' *Studies in Adult Education,* April 1972, 57–62.

Tulving, E. 'The Effects of Presentation and Recall of Materials in Free-Recall Learning.' *Journal of Verbal Learning and Verbal Behaviour* **6,** 175–84.

von Restorff, H. 'Über die Wirkung von Bereichsbildungen im Spurenfeld.' *Psychologische Forschung* **18,** 299–342.

Wagner, D. 'Memories of Morocco: the influence of age, schooling and environment on memory.' *Cognitive Psychology* **10,** 1–28. 1978.

Yates, F. A. *The Art of Memory.* London: Routledge & Kegan Paul, 1966; Ark, 1984.

Index